Heart Chakra 101: The Bridge
Copyright © 2025 by Dr. Constance Santego.

Copy Editor & Interior Design: Constance Santego
Book Layout: ©2017 BookDesignTemplates.com

Ordering Information:
Quantity sales. Special discounts are available on quantity purchases by corporations, associations, and others. For details, contact the "Special Sales Department" at the address above.

Trade Paperback ISBN: 978-1-990062-92-6
Ebook ISBN 978-1-990062-93-3
Created and published In Canada. Printed and bound in the United States of America

First Edition
Published by Maximillian Enterprises
Kelowna, BC Canada
www.constancesantego.ca

Heart Chakra 101: The Bridge

"Healing the Bridge Between Body and Soul."
(Vol I)

Dr. Constance Santego

Maximillian Enterprises
Kelowna, BC

Dedication

For the healers, seekers, and teachers who hold space for others with compassion. May this guide help your own heart remain nourished, even as you help others heal theirs.

— Dr. Constance Santego

ALSO BY DR. CONSTANCE SANTEGO

NOVELS
Illegitimate Grace
Ashcroft Hollow

Okanagan Trilogy:
Beneath the Vineyards
Under the Okanagan Sun
Guardian of the Lake

The Nine Spiritual Gifts Series:
Journey of a Soul – (Vol 1 Michael)
Language of a Soul – (Vol 2 Gabriel)
Prophecy of a Soul – (Vol 3 Bath Kol)
Healing of a Soul – (Vol 4 Raphael)
Miracles of a Soul – (Vol 5 Hamied)
Knowledge of a Soul – (Vol 6 Raziel)
Wisdom of a Soul – (Vol 7 Uriel)
Faith of a Soul – (Vol 8 Pistis Sophia)

NONFICTION
The Intuitive Life, The Gift Of Prophecy, Third Edition
Fairy Tales, Dreams And Reality… Where Are You On Your Path? Second Edition
Your Persona… The Mask You Wear
Archangel Michael's Soul Retrieval Guide
Tesla And The Future Of Energy Medicine
Beyond Tesla: Advancing The Science Of Energy Healing
Tesla's Code: Mastering Energy, Frequency, And Creative Power
Beyond The Mind: Harnessing The Power Of Astral Projection For Creative Awakening
Bend, Don't Break: Finding Your Way Back To Abundance
Ring Therapy: A Guide To Healing And Balance
Ring Therapy Pocket Guide
Floraopathy™: The Art And Science Of Vibrational Healing With Essential Oils
Dear Older Me: A Memoir… Of Sorts
It's Just Like Poker: A Spiritual Guide To Playing The Cards Life Deals You
Signs And Meanings: What The Feet Reveal About Health, Stress, And The Body's Story
Auricions: Unlocking Subconscious Healing Through Quantum Medicine
Quick Fix Acupressure Method
Manifestation – The DREAM Method in 5 Steps
Confidence- Mastering the Dream Method

REIKI WISDOM, SERIES:
Angelic Lifestyle, a Vibrant Lifestyle
Angelic Lifestyle 42-Day Energy Cleanse
Reiki and the Power of The Joint Points: Unlocking Energy Pathways for Healing (Vol I)
Reiki and Karmic Healing: Releasing Patterns From Past Lives (Vol II)
Reiki and the Five Elements (Vol III)
Secrets of a Healer, Magic Of Reiki
The Reiki Master's Manual

CHAKRA SERIES:
Heart Chakra 101: The Bridge
Root Chakra 101: Building Safety, Survival, Foundation
Sacral Chakra 101: Creativity, Pleasure, Emotions
Solar Plexus Chakra 101: Power, Confidence, Will
Throat Chakra 101: Truth, Voice, Self-Expression
Third Eye Chakra 10: Intuition, Vision, Insight
Crown Chakra 10: Spiritual Connection, Transcendence.

SECRETS OF A HEALER, SERIES:
Magic Of Aromatherapy (Vol I)
Magic Of Reflexology (Vol II)
Magic Of The Gifts (Vol III)
Magic Of Muscle Testing (Vol IV)
Magic Of Iridology (Vol V)
Magic Of Massage (Vol VI)
Magic Of Hypnotherapy (Vol VII)
Magic Of Reiki (Vol VIII)
Magic Of Advanced Aromatherapy (Vol IX)
Magic Of Esthetics (Vol X)
The Reiki Master's Manual (Vol XI)

ADULT COLORING JOURNALS
SERIES-ZEN COLORING:
Quantum Energy and Mindful Living Journal (Vol 1)
Reiki Energy Journal (Vol 2)
Nine Spiritual Gifts Journal (Vol 3)
I Forgive Journal (Vol 4)

FOR CHILDREN
I am Big Tonight. I Don't Need the Light
The Magic Elf Book: 25 Days of Surprises

COOKBOOK
My Favorite Recipes, with a Hint of Giggle

BUISNESS
How To Use ChatGPT For Authors: From Idea To Published Book
Scaling Beyond 6 Figures: Strategies For Health & Wellness Professionals
The Academypreneur's Playbook: Turn Knowledge Into A
Revenue-Generating School

HUMOR/GIFT BOOK
How Do You Like Your Eggs? Crack Into Your Personality, Yolk and All

Contents

Chapter 1 – Opening the Gate of the Heart

Why Healers Begin with the Heart

If you are holding this book, you may already be familiar with the word' *chakra,'* or perhaps it's new to you. Either way, imagine for a moment that your body is not just flesh and bone but also a field of living energy — pulsing, shifting, and communicating with every thought, feeling, and action you take.

Think of the last time you walked into a room where two people had just argued. Even if they stopped speaking the moment you entered, you could *feel* the tension in the air. Or remember a time when someone you love hugged you — that invisible sense of warmth and safety wasn't just physical; it was energy. We pick up these signals all the time, even when no words are spoken.

That subtle "something" you sense is what healers and practitioners refer to as your **energy field**. It's always moving, always responding — like a radio station tuned to the frequency of your inner state. Chakras are the main broadcasting towers within that system, shaping how you send and receive energy in every moment of your life.

This energy isn't random or floating around without purpose. It moves through special centers in your body called **chakras**. The Sanskrit word *chakra* means "wheel" or "disk," because you can picture them as spinning wheels of energy that keep things moving.

Each chakra is like a power center. It helps different parts of your life work smoothly — your body, your emotions, your thoughts, and even your sense of connection to something greater than yourself.

When these centers are open and balanced, your whole system works in harmony. You feel healthier, more at ease in your body, steadier in your emotions, and clearer in your mind. Life seems to flow.

But when one of these chakras is blocked or out of balance, it's like a kink in a garden hose — the energy can't flow freely. That's when stress, tension, sadness, or even physical problems can show up. In short, your energy system is the bridge between how you feel on the inside and how you experience life on the outside.

There are seven primary chakras, running from the base of your spine to the crown of your head. Each chakra governs different aspects of human experience: survival, creativity, personal power, love, communication, intuition, and spiritual connection. Together, they create a map of what it means to be human — body and spirit woven together.

Now, right in the middle of this system lies the **Heart Chakra, or Anahata**. It is more than just the "fourth chakra" in a sequence. It is the **gateway**, the bridge between your earthly needs and your spiritual aspirations. The lower chakras (Root, Sacral, Solar Plexus) ground you in the material world: food, safety, sexuality, and personal identity. The upper chakras (Throat, Third Eye, Crown) open you to realms of expression, vision, and divine connection.

But without the Heart, there is no union between the two; this is the chakra that allows you to bring **energy, life force, spirit, love, or consciousness into matter** *(however you name it)* — **and matter back into the unseen**. It is the place where human love meets divine love, where compassion melts boundaries, and where forgiveness creates freedom.

This is why many healers begin with the Heart. It is the **center of centers**, the place where your healing journey finds balance. To speak only of survival without love would be incomplete. To soar into spiritual insight without compassion would be ungrounded. The Heart Chakra is where healing begins because it is where separation ends.

When your heart is open, energy flows naturally. You feel connected — to yourself, to others, and to something greater. When your heart is closed, everything feels harder: relationships, self-worth, even your spiritual practice. That is why healers, Reiki practitioners, and seekers throughout time have placed so much emphasis on the heart as the true seat of the soul.

In this book, we will explore the many layers of Anahata — its history, hidden secrets, signs of imbalance, and the countless ways to bring it back into harmony. Whether you are completely new to chakras or a seasoned practitioner, beginning with the Heart will give you a foundation not only for understanding energy, but also for embodying it in the most essential way: **through love**.

WANT TO SEE IT IN ACTION?...
Watch this video for more insight and tips on Energy.

Watch it here: Proof of Energy
https://youtu.be/jnZAOGYWy2M and
https://youtu.be/0mEXbz11LME

*REMINDER: A **chakra** is like a little **invisible wheel of energy** inside your body. You can't see it the way you see your hands or feet, but you can feel it — like when your heart feels warm when you're happy, or your stomach feels tight when you're worried.*

Each chakra helps a different part of you work — your body, your feelings, your thoughts, and even how you connect with others. When a chakra is working well, it's like the wheel is spinning smoothly and everything feels good. But if it slows down or gets stuck, you might feel sad, tired, or even get a tummy ache or feel heavy in your chest.

*Chakras are like your body's **energy helpers**. When they're balanced, life feels easier, brighter, and more full of love.*

What Is a Chakra?

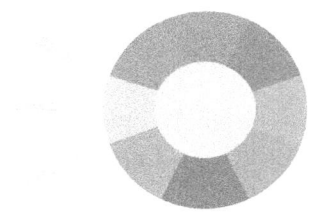

A chakra is like a little invisible wheel of energy inside your body.

Each chakra helps a different part of you work — your body, your feelings, your thoughts, and even how you connect with others.

When they're balanced, life feels easier, brighter, and more full of love.

The Unique Role of Anahata in Healing

The Heart Chakra is called **Anahata** in Sanskrit, a word that means *"unstruck sound."* Ancient teachers used this phrase to describe a vibration so pure it exists without conflict — a steady resonance of harmony and love. Over time, this understanding of the heart as a center of wholeness has been carried through many spiritual and healing traditions.

Chakras are not only part of yoga and meditation; similar ideas appear across cultures. In **Reiki**, the chakras are seen as key points where universal energy flows through the body. In **Ayurveda**, they are tied to health, diet, and the subtle body. In **Traditional Chinese Medicine**, while not called chakras, the meridians and energy centers reflect the same truth — that the body, mind, and emotions are linked through currents of energy. Even modern approaches such as **sound therapy, aromatherapy, crystal healing, hypnosis, and energy psychology** draw from chakra principles, whether they name them or not.

Within this wide landscape of healing, the Heart Chakra holds a special place. It is often described as the **center of the healer's touch** — the place where compassion, intention, and universal energy meet. When you place your hands on your chest in self-healing or on a client in a Reiki session, it is not only the technique that matters. What creates change is the **quality of energy** flowing through your heart.

When Anahata is open and balanced, the practitioner becomes a clear channel, allowing energy to move freely without distortion. At the same time, it creates a field of safety and trust, because people can always feel when healing is offered with genuine care. In this way, the Heart Chakra becomes a bridge between the **universal life force** and the **personal experience**

of love and connection. A session is no longer just treatment — it becomes a space of harmony and wholeness.

ENVISIONING ANAHATA

Close your eyes for a moment and bring your awareness to the center of your chest, right at your sternum. Imagine a **soft green light** glowing there, warm and steady, like sunlight streaming through spring leaves. With each breath in, this light grows brighter; with each breath out, it gently expands, filling your chest with ease.

Now, picture this light taking shape as a **lotus flower** with twelve petals. Each petal glows with green radiance, shimmering slightly as if touched by starlight. At the very center of the lotus, see **two triangles overlapping** — one pointing upward, one pointing downward — forming a harmonious six-pointed star.

From this star, a pulse of light radiates outward in every direction. Feel it flowing forward through your chest, backward between your shoulder blades, and outward into the space around you. This is the heart of Anahata — a center of balance, compassion, and harmony.

Take a few moments to simply breathe here. Notice how the light feels as it radiates through you. Perhaps it feels like warmth, or peace, or a gentle hum. This is not just your imagination; this is you tuning into the living energy of your heart chakra.

When you are ready, carry this vision of Anahata with you — a lotus of green light, glowing steadily at the center of your being, reminding you that love and balance are always within reach.

That is *Anahata*: not just a chakra, but a **living lotus of green light and balance**, pulsing quietly at the center of your being.

What Is Sanskrit and Why Does It Matter for Chakras?

To truly understand the chakras, we must begin with the language in which they were first described: **Sanskrit**.

Sanskrit is one of the world's oldest living languages, with roots stretching back over 3,500 years in ancient India. It is the language of the **Vedas** — some of humanity's earliest sacred texts — as well as the **Upanishads** and **Tantric scriptures**, writings that explore everything from philosophy and cosmology to medicine, ritual, and meditation.

Unlike most languages that change with time and usage, Sanskrit was preserved with extraordinary care. For thousands of years, students memorized entire scriptures word for word, sound for sound, passing them down through precise oral tradition before they were ever written. This dedication wasn't only about preserving knowledge — it was about preserving vibration.

In the ancient worldview, Sanskrit was considered a **sacred language of sound and energy**. Each syllable was believed to carry not just meaning, but a vibration that resonated with the fabric of creation itself. To speak Sanskrit was to align your voice with cosmic frequencies. To chant it was to awaken the body, mind, and spirit into harmony with universal truth.

This is why **mantras** (sacred sounds or phrases) are so central in yogic and tantric practice. When people chanted in Sanskrit, they weren't simply reciting words — they were striking a tuning fork that resonated with specific layers of consciousness. A mantra wasn't just heard; it was felt, moving through the body's subtle energy channels, stirring awareness, and activating change.

The chakras, described in these traditions, were always given **Sanskrit names** and paired with a **seed sound** (*bija mantra*). These weren't random labels. Each name was chosen to reflect the essence of the energy center itself, capturing its qualities in both meaning and vibration.

- *Muladhara* (Root Chakra) means "foundation" or "support," describing our grounding in the physical world.
- *Svadhisthana* (Sacral Chakra) means "dwelling place of the self," pointing to creativity and fluidity.
- *Manipura* (Solar Plexus) means "city of jewels," reflecting power and inner radiance.
- *Anahata* (Heart Chakra), as we will soon explore, means *"unstruck, unhurt, unbeaten"* — the eternal sound of harmony and love that is untouched by conflict.

When you speak or chant these words, you are not only naming a chakra — you are **calling forth its vibration**, aligning yourself with the ancient current of energy it represents.

This is the gift of Sanskrit: it gives us more than vocabulary. It gives us a bridge into the **energetic reality** the chakras describe, a way to experience them not only as concepts, but as living vibrations within our own body.

SANSKRIT AND THE BIBLE: IS THERE A CONNECTION?

Sanskrit and Biblical Hebrew (the original language of much of the Old Testament) are both **ancient sacred languages** — each treated as holy, each believed to carry divine power through sound.

- **Sanskrit** was the language of the Vedas, Upanishads, and Tantric texts in India. It was passed down orally with absolute precision for thousands of years before being written. Its sounds (mantras) were considered vibrations of creation itself.
- **Biblical Hebrew** was the language of Jewish scripture, where letters and words were believed to hold creative force. In Jewish mysticism (Kabbalah), each Hebrew letter carried spiritual energy, and the act of speaking scripture was seen as invoking divine presence.

Both traditions saw **sound as sacred** — not just a way of communicating, but a way of aligning with God or universal truth.

FROM BASICS TO DISCOVERY

Now that you've seen the essentials of the Heart Chakra, remember that this is only the beginning. These are the roots — the colors, the symbols, the qualities, and the simple practices that anyone can try. They are important because they give us language and structure, a way to name what we feel in our bodies and in our lives.

But the Heart Chakra, or Anahata, is much more than a list of correspondences or a set of exercises. It is a **gateway of discovery**. Hidden within this chakra are stories, ancient teachings, and modern applications that most people never explore. Beyond the basics lie the subtle dimensions — the history, the myths, the cross-cultural wisdom, and the advanced healing methods that deepen our understanding of the heart's energy.

That is what this book is about. *Heart Chakra 101* will take you further than a chart or a quick meditation. Together, we will step into the mysteries of Anahata:

- How it has been understood across spiritual traditions
- The hidden qualities and shadow sides that shape our relationships and inner life
- Practical tools for practitioners, from Reiki to sound healing to modern energy psychology
- And the deeper, often unspoken, lessons of love, compassion, and balance that this chakra holds

Think of what you've just read as **opening the door**. In the chapters ahead, we will walk through it — exploring not only what the Heart Chakra *is*, but also what it *asks of us* as healers, seekers, and human beings.

SETTING AN INTENTION FOR HEART-CENTERED PRACTICE

Information on its own can stay in the mind. But when we set an intention, knowledge becomes a living practice. The Heart Chakra responds most powerfully to sincerity, openness, and the willingness to love — not just others, but yourself.

Before you go further into this book, I invite you to set a personal intention for your journey with Anahata. This doesn't need to be complicated. Simply pause, take a deep breath, and place your hand over the center of your chest.

Ask yourself:

- *"What do I most need in my heart right now?"*
- *"What quality of love or compassion do I want to invite into my life as I learn about this chakra?"*

Let the answer rise naturally. It may be a single word, like **forgiveness**, **trust**, **joy**, or **peace**. Or it may be a phrase, such as:

- *"I am open to receiving love as easily as I give it."*
- *"I allow my heart to be a safe and healing place."*
- *"I choose to live from love, not fear."*

Hold this intention gently in your awareness as you continue through these chapters. Think of it as a lantern lighting your way. Each practice, story, and teaching you encounter will have a deeper impact when it flows through the intention of your own heart.

Chapter 2 – Foundations of Anahata

Heart Chakra Basics: A Gentle Recap

Before we journey deeper into the mysteries of the Heart Chakra, let's pause to review the essentials. If you've never studied chakras before, don't worry — this will give you a foundation. And if you already have some experience, think of this as a refreshing moment to return to the basics.

The **Sanskrit name** for the Heart Chakra is *Anahata*, which translates to *"unstruck, unhurt, unbeaten."* This word points to something very special — a vibration of love that exists beyond conflict, beyond pain, a sound of harmony that continues whether life feels heavy or light.

The Heart Chakra is often shown as a **green, twelve-petaled lotus**, with two intersecting triangles forming a star. The green represents growth and healing, while the triangles symbolize balance — masculine and feminine, earthly and divine, giving and receiving.

You'll find this chakra at the **center of your chest**, right at the sternum. It is the fourth of the seven main chakras, opening both forward and backward. Its frequency resonates at **639 Hz**, a vibration often used in music and sound healing to open the heart to love and connection.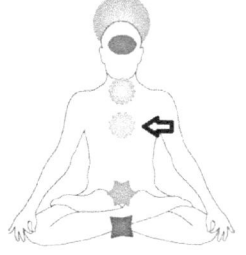

What the Heart Chakra Represents

The Heart Chakra is the energy of **love, compassion, balance, and forgiveness**. It is your inner home of:

- Romance and tenderness, but also jealousy when wounded
- Connection to others and to yourself
- Trust, joy, and gratitude
- The pure source of love

When your heart energy is flowing freely, you feel warm, sincere, and at peace. You have compassion for yourself and for others, and you feel connected to life in a way that is steady and real.

HOW THE HEART CHAKRA AFFECTS THE BODY

This chakra is connected to your **heart, lungs, and immune system**, and is closely tied to the **thymus gland**. When the energy here is balanced, your body naturally supports vitality and harmony.

But when it is blocked or out of balance, the effects can show up physically, emotionally, and even spiritually.

- **Physical signs** may include chest pain, high or low blood pressure, palpitations, poor immunity, asthma, breast cancer, or chronic fatigue.
- **Emotional and mental signs** may look like grief, envy, dissatisfaction, self-doubt, blame, coldness, or being overly dependent on others for love and recognition.
- **Spiritual imbalance** may feel like being cut off from divine love, or not being able to sense the loving presence of something greater.

SIMPLE WAYS TO BALANCE YOUR HEART CHAKRA

Healing the Heart Chakra doesn't have to be complicated.
Small, daily practices can open it gently and steadily:

- **Affirmations:** Say to yourself, *"I love myself. I love others. Others love me. My heart radiates light and love."*
- **Aromatherapy:** Try rose, eucalyptus, pine, marjoram, or yarrow to soothe and uplift the heart.
- **Crystals:** Work with rose quartz, jade, emerald, or malachite. Hold them, wear them, or place them over your chest.
- **Color Therapy:** Surround yourself with green — clothes, candles, foods, plants, and time in nature.
- **Sound:** Listen to music tuned to 639 Hz, chant "YAM," or use a tuning fork near your chest.
- **Meditation:** Light a green candle, breathe deeply, and imagine your chest glowing with healing green light.
- **Reiki:** Place your hands gently on your chest, front and back, to channel healing energy.
- **Self-healing rituals:** Hug someone (or a favorite pillow or pet), walk in the forest, breathe deeply in the wind, or simply sit in gratitude.

This is just the starting point. These practices are like opening the door to your heart. In the chapters ahead, we'll step through that door together and explore what lies beyond — the hidden history of Anahata, deeper healing practices, and advanced insights that can transform not only your own heart, but the way you share healing with others.

Cross-Cultural Perspectives on the Heart Chakra

Though the word *chakra* comes from Sanskrit and its roots lie in Indian philosophy, the wisdom of the heart as a center of love, balance, and higher connection is found across many cultures. By exploring these cross-cultural perspectives, we see that Anahata is not just an idea from one tradition — it is a **universal truth recognized in many different languages of healing and spirituality.**

HINDU & YOGIC TRADITIONS: THE ORIGINAL ANAHATA

In the Tantric and yogic scriptures of India, the Heart Chakra is described as a **twelve-petaled green lotus** with two intersecting triangles forming a six-pointed star. Its bija (seed sound) is **YAM**, and its essence is *Anahata*, the "unstruck sound."

Anahata was seen as the **gateway between the lower and higher chakras**, uniting survival and desire with spiritual awakening. Yogis meditated on this chakra to dissolve emotional wounds, awaken compassion, and hear the subtle inner sound of the soul. It was not only about love for others but about realizing *Atman* — the divine Self within.

TIBETAN BUDDHISM: CHANNELS, WINDS, AND COMPASSION

In Tibetan Buddhism, chakras are not described in exactly the same way as in Hindu Tantra, but there is a close parallel through the system of **channels (tsa), winds (lung), and drops (tigle).**

The heart center is described as a **subtle channel wheel** where winds of energy gather. Practitioners use advanced meditation techniques to direct these winds into the central channel at the heart, dissolving ego and awakening *bodhicitta* — the mind of compassion.

For Tibetan practitioners, the heart center is where the **clear light of awareness** is realized, the pure state of mind beyond grasping. This connects beautifully with Anahata's meaning: the sound that is unstruck, untouched by conflict.

KABBALAH: TIFERET, THE HEART OF THE TREE OF LIFE

In Jewish mysticism, or Kabbalah, there is no chakra system, but there is a profound parallel. On the **Tree of Life**, the sefirah (sphere) called **Tiferet** — meaning "beauty" or "harmony" — sits at the very center, like a heart.

Tiferet represents the balance between the upper and lower sefirot, just as the Heart Chakra balances the upper and lower chakras. It is the place of compassion, love, and the harmonizing of opposites — mercy and judgment, spirit and matter, heaven and earth. Mystics describe it as the point where divine light flows into human love, mirroring the unifying role of Anahata.

CHINESE MEDICINE: THE HEART AND LUNG MERIDIANS

In Traditional Chinese Medicine (TCM), chakras are not part of the system, yet the idea of the heart as a spiritual and physical center is clear. The **Heart Meridian** is called the "Emperor" of the body, responsible for consciousness, joy, and circulation. If the heart is disturbed, both emotions and health falter.

The **Lung Meridian**, closely tied to breath, also connects to grief and letting go — themes that resonate strongly with the Heart Chakra's lessons of forgiveness and release.

Practices like **qigong and acupuncture** emphasize balance between these meridians, which parallels the way chakra balancing restores harmony in energy flow. Both traditions agree: the health of the heart is more than physical; it is emotional and spiritual.

CHRISTIAN MYSTICISM: THE HEART OF CHRIST-CONSCIOUSNESS

Within Christian mystical tradition, the heart is often described as the **dwelling place of Christ** and the seat of divine love. Saints and mystics wrote about the "Sacred Heart," radiant with compassion, mercy, and forgiveness.

Christ-consciousness was experienced as a burning love within the heart that transformed the soul and opened the way to union with God. This resonates deeply with Anahata's qualities of unconditional love, unity, and forgiveness.

For Christian mystics, prayer and contemplation were ways of **awakening the heart** to God's presence — not unlike meditation or mantra practice in Eastern traditions.

A UNIVERSAL THREAD

Though each culture speaks in its own language — Sanskrit mantras, Tibetan winds, Hebrew sefirot, Chinese meridians, or Christian devotion — the message is the same:

- The heart is more than a physical organ.
- It is a **spiritual center** of love, harmony, and balance.
- It is the **bridge** where human experience touches the divine.

This universal recognition shows us that the Heart Chakra is not bound to one path. Whether through yoga, Reiki, prayer, or qigong, all traditions invite us to open the heart — for it is here that healing, compassion, and true connection are born.

WHY THIS MATTERS FOR THE HEART CHAKRA

The connection between Sanskrit and the Bible isn't about shared words — it's about a **shared reverence for sound as divine**. Both traditions teach that the spoken word carries spiritual power:

- In Sanskrit, the *bija mantra* "YAM" resonates with Anahata, awakening love and compassion.
- In the Bible, Proverbs 18:21 declares: *"Life and death are in the power of the tongue."*

Both affirm that the **heart and voice are connected** — what we speak shapes our inner world and the world around us.

Origins & Hidden History of Anahata

Most people today hear the word *chakra* in a yoga class or a wellness workshop. But what if I told you that the Heart Chakra carries a story much older — and far more mysterious — than you've ever been taught?

THE FORGOTTEN MEANING OF ANAHATA

Anahata, the Sanskrit name for the Heart Chakra, means "the unstruck sound." What is an unstruck sound? It is a vibration that arises without cause — a tone beyond the reach of human ears, said to echo eternally in the silence of the soul.

Ancient yogis described this resonance as the secret music of the universe. Unlike the bang of a drum or the pluck of a string, it is the sound that is *always there*, whether or not we notice. To listen for Anahata was to listen for the eternal heartbeat beneath creation itself — the pulse of love that endures untouched by conflict, fear, or time.

THE HIDDEN SYMBOLISM

Tantric texts describe the Heart Chakra as a lotus with twelve petals. To the untrained eye, it is just a symbol — but each petal holds a vibration, a divine quality of the heart: compassion, forgiveness, patience, joy. Meditating on these petals was a way to awaken those very virtues within yourself.

At the center of the lotus lies the six-pointed star: two interlocking triangles. One rises, pointing to heaven; one descends, pointing to earth. Together they mark the union of opposites — masculine and feminine, human and divine, the visible and the unseen. The heart was never just a chakra; it was a doorway.

PARALLELS FEW PEOPLE SPEAK OF

What makes Anahata's history even more magical is how its echoes appear across the world:

- In India, creation begins with sound — the sacred syllable *OM.*
- In the Bible, creation begins with a Word: *"In the beginning was the Word, and the Word was with God, and the Word was God."*
- In mystical Judaism, the heart of the Tree of Life is Tiferet — beauty, harmony, the radiant center.
- In Sufi tradition, the *qalb* (heart) is polished through remembrance until it reflects the light of the Divine.

Different cultures, different languages, yet the same secret: the heart is not just flesh and blood, but a **gateway to the eternal.**

WHAT HISTORY DOESN'T TELL YOU

The textbooks may present chakras as tidy diagrams or psychological models, but hidden in ancient chants, in sacred names, and in cross-cultural echoes is something far more mystical:

- That there is a sound of the heart which cannot be heard but only felt.
- That symbols like the lotus and the hexagram are not art, but maps to higher states of consciousness.
- That the human heart has always been seen — from Tantra to Christianity to Sufism — as the meeting place of the human and the divine.

This is the history most people never hear. And it is why the Heart Chakra is not just the fourth chakra, but the **living bridge between worlds.**

The Symbolism of the Heart Chakra

The traditional symbol of Anahata carries layers of meaning that go far beyond its outer beauty.

Comparison:

- **The Twelve Petals (Virtues):** The *finished flower* — qualities of a balanced, awakened heart.
- **The Twelve Petals as Vrittis:** The *garden in progress* — where weeds (negative thought-forms) are transformed into blossoms (virtues) through awareness.

THE TWELVE PETALS (VIRTUES / DIVINE QUALITIES)

- **Focus:** These are the **positive heart qualities** — joy, peace, clarity, love, compassion, forgiveness, patience, kindness, harmony, empathy, understanding, bliss.
- **Tone:** They describe what the awakened heart *naturally expresses* when in balance.
- **Use:** These petals are often meditated on as *virtues to cultivate,* like opening flowers within the heart.
- **Example:** When you focus on the petal of "compassion," you invite that quality to bloom more fully in your life.

This lens is about the **light side** of the heart: what we aspire to, what we grow into, and what love looks like when whole.

The Twelve Petals of the Heart Chakra

In Tantric symbolism, Anahata is not merely a circle or star — it is a **lotus with twelve radiant petals.** Each petal vibrates with a quality of the awakened heart. To meditate on these petals was to awaken them within yourself, layer by layer, like unlocking the chambers of a sacred temple.

The petals are often described as virtues, but they are more than abstract qualities — they are living frequencies of the heart. Together, they form a mandala of love, showing us twelve ways to embody divine connection.

1. Joy (Ānanda)

- Joy is the natural state of the heart when it is free from fear.
- It is not tied to circumstance, but bubbles up like a spring of light within.

- Meditating on this petal reminds us that joy is not earned, it is remembered.

2. Peace (Śānti)

- Peace is the calm that arises when we stop resisting life.
- It is the steady rhythm beneath the chaos, the silence between the notes.
- This petal softens the nervous system and teaches us to rest in being.

3. Clarity (Viveka)

- Clarity is the heart's wisdom that cuts through confusion.
- When balanced, Anahata sees people and situations clearly — without projection or illusion.
- It brings truth that feels both sharp and compassionate.

4. Love (Prema)

- Love here is not romantic possession, but the unconditional flow that arises when the heart is open.
- It is the magnetic force that unites all life.
- This petal reminds us: love is not something we do, it is something we are.

5. Patience (Kṣānti)

- Patience is the spaciousness of the heart.
- It allows growth, forgiveness, and healing to unfold in their own timing.
- This petal trains us to trust the process instead of forcing outcomes.

6. Kindness (Maitrī)

- Kindness is love made visible in small acts.
- It is the hand extended, the gentle word spoken, the smile offered freely.
- This petal opens us to everyday miracles of compassion.

7. Understanding (Bodha)

- Understanding is empathy deepened into wisdom.
- It asks us to see not only *what* someone feels, but *why*.
- This petal dissolves judgment and allows true connection.

8. Harmony (Sāmya)

- Harmony is balance — of giving and receiving, of inner and outer, of self and other.
- It is the heart's ability to find resonance, like notes blending in a chord.
- This petal guides relationships into flow instead of friction.

9. Empathy (Anukampā)

- Empathy is the willingness to feel with another without losing your own center.
- It is the bridge of shared humanity that says, *"I see you, I feel you, I am with you."*
- This petal creates a safe space for healing.

10. Compassion (Karunā)

- Compassion is empathy with action.
- It is the choice to alleviate suffering where we can, and to hold loving presence where we cannot.
- This petal is the heart's highest expression of service.

11. Forgiveness (Kṣamā)

- Forgiveness is the key that unchains the heart from the past.
- It does not erase the wound, but it releases the hold it has on us.
- This petal opens the way for new love to flow where bitterness once lived.

12. Bliss (Ānanda-Maya)

- Bliss is the ultimate flowering of the heart.
- It is the merging of human and divine love, the ecstasy of unity.
- This petal represents the crown of Anahata — the heart as a temple of infinite light.

The Living Lotus

When meditated on together, the twelve petals are like twelve doors into one chamber — the sacred space of unconditional love. They remind us that the awakened heart is not one-dimensional. It is vast, radiant, and multi-faceted — a lotus of living light.

THE TWELVE PETALS AS VRITTIS (MENTAL MODIFICATIONS / THOUGHT-FORMS)

In classical Tantra, the twelve petals of Anahata were not described only as virtues. Each petal was also linked to a **vritti** — a subtle mental modification, or state of mind, that could either bind or free the heart. These vrittis are the patterns we carry: hopes and despairs, attachments and aversions, longings and fears.

- **Focus:** In classical Tantra, the petals also symbolized **vrittis** — mental patterns or states of mind that can distort the heart.
- **Tone:** Instead of just naming virtues, these vrittis include both light and shadow, like "hope" vs. "despair," "faith" vs. "doubt," "compassion" vs. "cruelty."
- **Use:** The petals here are seen as **arenas of transformation** — where raw human emotions and thoughts are purified into their divine form through awareness, mantra, or meditation.
- **Example:** The petal of "hope" may also carry the shadow of "despair." By bringing presence to despair, it can transmute into true faith.

This lens is about the **alchemical side** of the heart: where human struggle is transformed into divine quality.

To meditate on the petals was not just to cultivate divine qualities, but to **transform these thought-forms** — refining raw human emotions into awakened states. In this way, the heart becomes the crucible where shadow and light are alchemized into wholeness.

The Twelve Petals as Vrittis

1. **Hope (Āśā)**

   - **Shadow:** Expectation that clings, setting us up for disappointment.
   - **Light:** Trust that life unfolds in the right timing. Hope matures into faith.

2. **Anxiety (Cintā)**

   - **Shadow:** The restless mind that worries endlessly.
   - **Light:** When calmed, this sharp awareness becomes discernment and clarity.

3. **Longing (Cintāyā)**

- **Shadow:** Desire that feels like a void, always grasping for more.
- **Light:** Becomes devotion — a yearning for truth and connection rather than possession.

4. **Possessiveness (Mamata)**

- **Shadow:** Love distorted into ownership.
- **Light:** Transforms into care without control, nurturing without grasping.

5. **Arrogance (Dambha)**

- **Shadow:** The pride that shuts out humility.
- **Light:** Refined into confidence rooted in love, not superiority.

6. **Discrimination (Viṣāda)**

- **Shadow:** Judgment that divides, harsh criticism of self or others.
- **Light:** Becomes discernment — the wisdom to see truth clearly without cruelty.

7. **Delusion (Moha)**

- **Shadow:** Being trapped in illusion, mistaking appearance for essence.
- **Light:** Awakens into clarity — seeing through illusion into deeper truth.

8. **Jealousy (Irṣyā)**

- **Shadow:** Fear of losing love, or resentment at another's joy.

- **Light:** Transforms into inspiration — letting another's success remind us of our own potential.

9. **Lust (Kāma)**

- **Shadow:** Desire that uses rather than honors.
- **Light:** Blossoms into sacred intimacy, where passion is an expression of love.

10. **Fraud/Deceit (Kapaṭa)**

- **Shadow:** Hiding truth, wearing masks to gain approval.
- **Light:** Opens into authenticity — the courage to be seen as we are.

11. **Defiance (Vitarka)**

- **Shadow:** Rebellion born of fear or stubbornness.
- **Light:** Transforms into strength of conviction, the power to stand for truth.

12. **Selfishness (Anavasāda)**

- **Shadow:** Closing the heart, serving only one's own needs.
- **Light:** Evolves into self-love that overflows naturally into service.

The Alchemy of Vrittis

These vrittis remind us that the heart is not only a place of sweetness. It is also where we wrestle with the messiness of human emotions. Each petal is a threshold: we can remain in the shadow of jealousy, grief, or arrogance — or we can cross into their higher expressions of inspiration, compassion, or humility.

To meditate on the vrittis is to practice **heart alchemy** — transforming the raw metal of emotion into the gold of awakened love.

The Intersecting Triangles of Anahata

At the very center of the Heart Chakra lotus lies a six-pointed star — two triangles, one pointing upward and the other downward, perfectly overlapping. To ancient seers, this was more than geometry; it was the heart's deepest truth drawn in symbol.

The Upward Triangle – Shiva

- Points to the sky.
- Represents the divine masculine, rising energy, fire, and transcendence.

Symbolizes spirit's journey upward — the call to expand, evolve, and return to the Source.

The Downward Triangle – Shakti

- Points to the earth.
- Represents the divine feminine, grounding energy, water, and creation.
- Symbolizes matter's journey downward — spirit descending into form, life taking root in the physical world.

WHO ARE SHIVA AND SHAKTI?

In the myths of India, long before chakras were drawn in colorful charts, sages spoke of two cosmic lovers: **Shiva** and **Shakti.**

- **Shiva** is pure consciousness. Imagine the vast sky — endless, still, unchanging. Shiva is the silent witness, the eternal awareness behind all things. He does not act; he simply *is.*
- **Shakti** is pure energy. Imagine the rivers rushing, the earth blossoming, the stars burning, your own heartbeat pulsing. Shakti is the creative force of life, the rhythm and movement that brings the universe into being. She is also called the Divine Mother.

In the stories, Shiva and Shakti are never truly apart. Consciousness (Shiva) without energy (Shakti) is still but empty. Energy (Shakti) without consciousness (Shiva) is wild but directionless. Only together do they create harmony.

The Union of Opposites

In Tantric teachings, the heart is the place where these two forces meet. Shiva's upward triangle (spirit rising) and Shakti's downward triangle (matter descending) overlap to form the six-pointed star at the center of Anahata.

Here, in your own chest, their eternal dance plays out:

- Your breath rises like Shiva, returning you to awareness.
- Your breath falls like Shakti, bringing you into the body.
- Every heartbeat is their rhythm, uniting silence and motion, heaven and earth.

When these triangles overlap, they form the hexagram — a sacred star that shows the union of above and below, heaven and earth, masculine and feminine, action and surrender.

In the heart, this union reveals itself in many ways:

- **Giving and Receiving:** The balance between offering love and allowing yourself to be loved.

- **Action and Rest:** Knowing when to move outward and when to soften inward.
- **Spiritual and Human:** Remembering that enlightenment is not about escaping the world but embodying love *within* it.

The triangles remind us that the heart does not choose sides. It is the place where opposites dissolve into wholeness.

MEDITATION WITH THE TRIANGLES

- Close your eyes and visualize the star glowing at your heart.
- See the upward triangle rising with your inhale, carrying you toward spirit.
- See the downward triangle grounding with your exhale, anchoring you to earth.
- Feel both movements happening together, until the two energies weave into balance — one star, one heart, one light.

THE GIFT OF THE TRIANGLES

The intersecting triangles remind us that the heart is not just about feeling — it is about integration. It teaches us that true healing comes not from choosing one polarity, but from embracing both. In Anahata, love is not divided. It is whole, radiant, and eternal.

The Six-Pointed Star of the Heart

When the upward triangle of Shiva and the downward triangle of Shakti meet, they create a six-pointed star — the hexagram. This symbol is more than geometry. It is the reminder that love is not passive; it is active, dynamic, and whole. True love requires balance — giving and receiving, expansion and grounding, heaven and earth woven into one radiant star.

In the Heart Chakra, the hexagram is the sacred seal of union. It shows that the awakened heart is not about choosing one path over another, but about weaving opposites into harmony.

SACRED GEOMETRY ACROSS TRADITIONS

The six-pointed star is not unique to Tantric imagery. Across time and culture, it has appeared as a sign of protection, balance, and divine union:

- **Hindu Tantra:** The star represents the eternal dance of **Shiva and Shakti**, consciousness and energy entwined. It is the cosmic marriage of the masculine and feminine, held within your own heart.
- **Jewish Mysticism:** Known as the **Star of David**, it symbolizes the covenant between humanity and the Divine, heaven descending into earth and earth rising toward heaven.
- **Alchemy:** The star was drawn to show the marriage of elements — **fire and water, sulfur and mercury** — a symbol of transformation where opposites fuse into a new creation.
- **The Human Body:** The star lives in us, too. It is the rhythm of **inhale and exhale**, the rise and fall of the chest, the expansion and contraction of the heartbeat. Every breath redraws the star inside you.

THE UNIVERSAL TRUTH OF THE STAR

Whether in Tantra, Kabbalah, alchemy, or embodied breath, the intersecting triangles whisper the same truth: **life is not about separation, but about union.** The heart is the place where this union becomes real — not as theory, but as lived experience.

Every time you breathe with awareness, every time you open to love, you reawaken the hexagram within. The star is not just a symbol on a page — it is alive in your chest, a glowing reminder that your heart was always meant to hold the whole.

Every line and petal of the Anahata symbol teaches that the heart is the place where unity is born.

THE HEXAGRAM AS MERKABA: THE HEART'S HIDDEN VEHICLE OF LIGHT

When most people see the six-pointed star in the Heart Chakra, they think of it as "just a symbol." But in esoteric traditions around the world, this same shape appears as something far more mysterious: the **Merkaba** (sometimes spelled Merkabah) — a vehicle of light for spiritual travel, protection, and ascension.

Origins of the Merkaba

The word *Merkaba* comes from Hebrew/Aramaic roots meaning "chariot" or "vehicle." In Jewish mysticism, the Merkaba was described as the **divine chariot of Ezekiel's vision** — a multi-layered, living geometry of light that could carry the soul into heavenly realms. Later esoteric teachings described the Merkaba as an interlocking pair of tetrahedrons spinning in opposite directions, creating a dynamic star-shaped field around the body.

Why It Appears in the Heart Chakra

The Heart Chakra's hexagram — the overlapping upward and downward triangles — mirrors the shape of the Merkaba exactly. In Tantric terms, it is the union of Shiva (spirit) and Shakti (matter). In mystical terms, it is the "engine" of the light body, spinning at the center of your being.

In this view, **the heart is not only an energy center but also a gateway**, where your physical and subtle bodies meet. When the heart is open, it generates a coherent electromagnetic field — a literal torus of energy around you — that can support higher states of awareness, intuitive travel, and spiritual protection.

Hidden Teachings of the Heart Gateway

Esoteric schools (from Kabbalah to Sufism to modern Merkaba meditation systems) have long taught that the heart is the launch point for:

- **Spiritual Travel / Astral Projection:** Using breath, sound, and visualization to "step" into higher dimensions while remaining anchored to the body.
- **Light Body Activation:** Awakening a subtle geometry of spinning fields around you, believed to enhance intuition, healing ability, and resilience.
- **Ascension Practices:** Not about "leaving Earth" but about embodying higher consciousness here and now, radiating it outward.

Practical Integration

You don't have to master advanced esoteric practices to benefit from this symbolism. Simply visualizing the **hexagram spinning gently in your heart center**, breathing slowly and evenly, can:

- Increase your sense of safety and protection.
- Heighten intuitive impressions during healing work.
- Create a feeling of expansion — as if your energy field is brighter and lighter.

As you grow in your practice, you may experience this star not just as a flat symbol but as a **three-dimensional Merkaba of light** surrounding your body — a living field of heart-centered energy that moves with you wherever you go.

The Heart as the Portal

Across traditions, the same hidden teaching repeats: **the heart is the gateway.** Whether in Tantric Anahata yoga, Jewish Merkaba mysticism, or modern energy work, the six-pointed star signals that your center of love is also your center of ascension. When you open your heart, you are not only more compassionate — you also step into your own vehicle of light.

THE CIRCLE AROUND THE LOTUS

At first glance, the circle around the Anahata lotus looks like a simple border — but in sacred geometry and Tantric symbolism, circles are never "just decoration." The circle is the most ancient symbol of wholeness. It has no beginning and no end, no corners, no divisions. It is the shape of the cosmos, the womb, the sun, the moon, and the eternal cycle of breath.

Eternity and Continuity

The circle enclosing the lotus shows that the heart is not a fragment but part of an eternal rhythm. Just as seasons turn, just as the inhale follows the exhale, the circle reminds us that life itself is cyclical — birth, death, and rebirth. In the center of that turning, the heart holds steady, like the still point of a wheel.

The Center of the Wheel of Life

The chakras are often envisioned as wheels (*chakras* literally means "spinning wheels"). The Heart Chakra's circle represents the central hub of this wheel — the axis around which all the spokes of life radiate. In yogic texts, the heart is described as the **pivot point** of the entire chakra system, balancing the three lower (earthly) and three higher (spiritual) centers. Without the circle of the heart, the wheel cannot turn smoothly.

Unity Within Diversity

A circle can hold infinite points along its edge, yet all are equal distance from the center. In the same way, the circle around the heart lotus symbolizes the unity of all beings, no matter how different their paths appear. Every relationship, every culture, every soul journey — all are drawn into connection through the heart's field of love.

Sacred Geometry and the Mandala

In Tantric diagrams (*yantras*), the enclosing circle is called the **bhupura** — the protective boundary of the sacred space. It sets the container for meditation, reminding the practitioner: *enter here, and you are stepping into the temple of the heart.* The heart is not just an organ of feeling; it is a mandala — a microcosm of the universe enclosed within your chest.

Practical Meditation with the Circle

Visualize the Heart Chakra lotus glowing in the center of your chest, surrounded by a luminous green circle. Imagine this circle expanding, becoming a sphere of light that surrounds your entire body. Inside this circle, you are safe, whole, and held in love. No wound, no fear, no separation can cross this sacred boundary. The circle reminds you that within the heart, you are complete.

THE COLOR GREEN (AND PINK) OF ANAHATA

When you close your eyes and visualize the Heart Chakra, the color most often seen is **green** — yet in modern healing traditions, **pink** also emerges as a companion color. These hues are not random. They carry deep meaning, both individually and together, offering a spectrum of what it means to love and to be loved.

Green: Healing, Renewal, Balance

- **The Color of Nature:** Green is the dominant color of forests, fields, and living plants. It reminds us that the heart, like the earth, has the power to regenerate. Even after a fire, new shoots of green rise. So too can the heart heal after loss.
- **Balance and Harmony:** In the color spectrum, green sits right in the middle. This reflects the role of the Heart Chakra as the midpoint of the seven chakras, balancing lower and higher energies.
- **Growth and Expansion:** Just as plants turn green when they receive sunlight, the heart flourishes when it receives love. Green symbolizes openness, growth, and the courage to reach for more.
- **Healing Frequency:** Many practitioners associate the vibration of green with restoration. To "bathe in green

light" through meditation or visualization is to invite balance back into body and spirit.

Green teaches us: love is the medicine of renewal.

Pink: Tenderness, Affection, Unconditional Love

- **The Color of Intimacy:** While green is expansive, pink draws us inward. It represents the soft, tender aspects of love — affection, nurturing, and the willingness to be vulnerable.
- **The Inner Child's Love:** Pink is often associated with innocence and the gentleness of being cared for. It awakens the part of us that longs to be held without judgment.
- **Compassionate Connection:** In modern healing traditions, pink resonates with the emotional warmth of the heart — the love that comforts, reassures, and accepts.
- **Unconditional Love:** Pink has been linked with the higher frequency of love that asks for nothing in return. It is the color of grace, forgiveness, and emotional openness.

Pink teaches us: love is tenderness without conditions.

Together: Green and Pink, Two Aspects of Love

When these two colors are visualized together, they reveal the full spectrum of the Heart Chakra:

- **Green as the Outer Field:** Healing, balance, and expansion — the universal love that connects us to nature, humanity, and life itself.
- **Pink as the Inner Flame:** Affection, vulnerability, and intimacy — the personal love that makes relationships meaningful and safe.

Some practitioners describe this as the *rose within the forest*: green holds the space of growth and renewal, while pink blossoms at the center as the pure expression of love's tenderness.

Green: The Fourth Color of the Rainbow

If you look at a rainbow — nature's own spectrum of light — green always appears in the center. It is the **fourth color**, just as the Heart Chakra is the fourth energy center in the human system.

This is not coincidence. Just as the rainbow balances between warm (red, orange, yellow) and cool (blue, indigo, violet) tones, the Heart Chakra balances between the **earthly chakras below** (root, sacral, solar plexus) and the **spiritual chakras above** (throat, third eye, crown). Green sits in the middle as the point of harmony.

- **Below Green:** Red, orange, and yellow root us in survival, creativity, and personal power.
- **Above Green:** Blue, indigo, and violet open us to expression, intuition, and divine awareness.
- **At Green:** Love bridges the two.

Just as the rainbow would be incomplete without green, so too is the human being incomplete without the heart's balance. Green shows us that love is not only an emotion but the **hinge of creation itself — the meeting point where matter and spirit touch.**

Meditation with Green and Pink

- Close your eyes and imagine your heart glowing with emerald-green light, expanding like a field around you.

- Now, in the center of this green light, see a soft pink flame glowing at your sternum — warm, gentle, unconditionally loving.
- Feel the two colors blending, green surrounding and protecting, pink softening and opening. Together, they create a full spectrum of heart energy: strong yet tender, expansive yet intimate.

MYTHS AND LESSER-KNOWN TRUTHS: WHY GREEN *AND* PINK BELONG TO THE HEART CHAKRA

When most people picture the Heart Chakra, they imagine it glowing green. This is true — but it is not the *only* truth. Many healers, mystics, and esoteric traditions also associate the heart with **pink light.** Why both? Let's explore the story.

The Green Heart: Growth, Balance, and Healing

Traditionally, Anahata is described as radiant green — the color of spring, new life, and renewal. Green is found at the **center of the visible spectrum**, balancing the warm reds and cool blues, just as the heart balances the lower and upper chakras.

- **Symbolism of green:** growth, harmony, restoration, and balance.
- **Healing resonance:** Green light is calming to the nervous system and is often used in color therapy to soothe tension and restore vitality.
- **Energetically:** Green represents the **universal, impersonal love** of compassion — love that expands outward to all beings.

This is why green is considered the "official" color of Anahata: it expresses balance, wholeness, and healing.

The Pink Heart: Unconditional Love and Tenderness

In modern energy healing, many practitioners also see or sense the Heart Chakra as **pink** — especially when working with crystals such as rose quartz or in meditations on unconditional love.

- **Symbolism of pink:** softness, nurturing, tenderness, emotional warmth.
- **Energetically:** Pink resonates with **personal, unconditional love** — the intimate, heart-to-heart connection that comforts and heals on a deeply emotional level.
- **Mystical truth:** Some clairvoyants describe green as the "outer layer" of Anahata and pink as its "inner flame," the tender core of pure love at the center of the heart field.

The Two Together

Instead of being contradictory, green and pink actually **complement each other**:

- Green represents balance, healing, and universal compassion.
- Pink represents softness, intimacy, and unconditional love.

Together, they mirror the dual role of the heart — to open outward in generosity (green) while also nurturing the deep, personal connections that make life meaningful (pink).

A Lesser-Known Teaching

Some esoteric traditions even say the heart has **two centers of light**:

- A **green lotus** radiating outward, connecting us to the web of life.
- A **pink flame** at the core, representing the soul's deepest capacity to love.

When both are activated, the heart becomes not only a center of compassion but also a radiant beacon of divine-human unity.

Why This Matters

Knowing that Anahata holds both colors reminds us that healing the heart requires **both dimensions of love**:

- The impersonal compassion that embraces humanity as a whole.
- The personal tenderness that makes us feel safe, cherished, and connected.

Your heart is not just one or the other — it is a living spectrum, where green and pink weave together to express the full beauty of love.

ANAHATA IN YOGIC PRACTICE

In the earliest Tantric and yogic traditions, the chakras were not viewed as physical organs, but as **meditation focal points**. Yogis would visualize each chakra while chanting specific seed sounds (*bija mantras*), using breath, sound, and visualization to awaken subtle layers of consciousness.

For Anahata, the bija mantra was **YAM**, a vibrational seed said to open the heart to compassion and dissolve barriers of resentment or fear. Meditating on the twelve-petaled lotus and chanting "YAM" allowed practitioners to feel a direct connection to the inner sound — the unstruck resonance of love.

The purpose was not merely to heal the body, but to **awaken spiritual consciousness**. The Heart Chakra was seen as the bridge between the lower, survival-oriented centers and the higher, spiritual centers of awareness. Opening Anahata meant opening the gateway to devotion, compassion, and the recognition of the divine in all beings.

The Inner Symbol of Anahata

At the very center of the Heart Chakra image, inside the six-pointed star and twelve-petaled lotus, is a **Sanskrit syllable**. This is the **bija mantra (seed sound)** of the Heart Chakra: **YAM (यं)**.

What YAM Represents

- **Vibrational Key:** YAM is the sacred sound said to "unlock" the Heart Chakra, aligning the practitioner with love, compassion, and balance.
- **Sound of the Heart:** Chanting YAM vibrates through the chest, lungs, and sternum — physically activating the energetic center of the heart.
- **Dissolver of Fear:** In Tantric and yogic texts, YAM was described as dissolving grief, fear, and heaviness, opening space for forgiveness and trust.
- **Link to Air Element:** Each chakra is tied to an element; Anahata is linked with **air** (vāyu). YAM is the sound that harmonizes breath, life force, and the flow of love through the heart.

The Seed Sound of Anahata: YAM

At the very center of the Heart Chakra's symbol lies not just geometry, but sound. In Tantric teachings, every chakra has a **bija mantra** — a "seed sound" said to carry the vibrational essence of that energy center. For Anahata, the bija is **YAM** (pronounced "Yahm," like *yawn* with an "m").

Why Sound Matters

In Sanskrit, sound is not just noise — it is vibration, frequency, and power. Ancient yogis taught that the universe itself began with sound (*OM*). In the same way, each chakra has its own vibrational key. Chanting that sound is like striking the exact note that opens a hidden lock.

For the Heart Chakra, YAM is that key. It carries the frequency of love, compassion, and harmony. When you chant YAM, you are not just speaking — you are tuning your heart to its original vibration of balance and connection.

The Power of YAM

- **Resonance in the Chest:** When chanted, YAM naturally vibrates in the sternum and lungs, directly stimulating the heart space.
- **Dissolving Fear:** Fear contracts the chest; YAM expands it. The sound helps release tension, grief, or guardedness.
- **Awakening Compassion:** YAM aligns the energy body with openness, empathy, and forgiveness.
- **Heart Coherence:** Regular chanting can bring breath, heartbeat, and nervous system into a more balanced rhythm.

How to Chant YAM

Step 1 – Prepare the Body

- Sit comfortably with a straight spine. Place your hands over your heart or rest them in your lap.
- Take 3–5 slow breaths, inhaling through the nose and exhaling through the mouth.

Step 2 – Focus on the Heart

- Visualize a glowing green light or lotus in the center of your chest. See it pulsing gently with your breath.

Step 3 – Chant the Sound

- Inhale deeply. As you exhale, chant: **YAAAAHHHHMmmmm…**
- Let the sound start strong in the open mouth ("Yah") and finish with lips closed, humming ("mmm").
- Feel the vibration spread across your sternum, into your ribs, and even into your back.

Step 4 – Repeat Rhythmically

- Continue chanting YAM 7, 12, or 108 times (using mala beads if you wish).
- With each round, imagine the green light in your chest glowing brighter and softer at the same time.

Step 5 – Silent Resonance

- After chanting, sit quietly. Listen inwardly. Feel the subtle vibration still humming in your chest, like the afterglow of a bell.

Ways to Use YAM in Practice

- **Morning Practice:** Chant YAM three times upon waking to open your day with love and balance.
- **Healing Sessions:** Reiki and energy practitioners can chant YAM silently or softly while holding the heart area, amplifying flow.
- **Emotional Release:** When feeling grief, fear, or jealousy, chant YAM until the chest softens.

- **Group Practice:** Chanting YAM in a circle magnifies the resonance — the sound waves align multiple hearts into harmony.
- **Meditation Integration:** Combine YAM with visualization — imagine each chant clearing the petals of the lotus, allowing the heart to bloom wider.

Heart-Centered Affirmation with YAM

"As I chant YAM, my heart opens. I am safe. I am love. I am connected to all beings."

THE DEITIES OF THE HEART CHAKRA

In traditional Tantric iconography, each chakra is presided over by specific deities who embody its qualities. These deities were never meant to be seen only as external gods, but also as **inner archetypes** — energies within us that awaken through meditation.

Ishvara – The Cosmic Self

- Ishvara is often depicted as the deity of Anahata, representing the **higher Self, the eternal witness, and divine presence within the heart.**
- In meditation, Ishvara is not just an external god, but the reminder that the heart is the **seat of the soul**, the place where the drop of individual consciousness touches the ocean of universal consciousness.

Kakini – The Feminine Guardian of the Heart

- Kakini is a Shakti goddess who presides over Anahata. She is portrayed with radiant green energy, holding symbols of devotion, purity, and love.

- She embodies **nurturing, protection, and devotion** —
  the qualities of the awakened heart when it is in service
  to life.
- As Shakti, she balances Ishvara, bringing energy,
  embodiment, and the nourishing touch of the divine
  feminine.

Together, Ishvara and Kakini remind us that the heart is the
union of **masculine and feminine, stillness and movement,
consciousness and energy.**

HEART DEITIES IN OTHER TRADITIONS

While only Tantra names Ishvara and Kakini explicitly, many
spiritual paths personify the heart through gods, goddesses, and
sacred figures. These parallels show a universal recognition of
the heart as the center of divine-human union.

Christian Mysticism

- The **Sacred Heart of Christ** is one of the most enduring
  heart symbols: a flaming, radiant heart representing
  unconditional love, sacrifice, and divine compassion.
- Mystics also spoke of the "indwelling Christ" in the
  heart, echoing the Tantric idea of the inner deity.

Hinduism & Bhakti Yoga

- The heart is often associated with **Krishna**, the god of
  divine love, and **Radha**, the soul's devotion. Their love
  story symbolizes the union of human longing (Radha)
  with divine love (Krishna).
- In another lens, the goddess **Lakshmi** embodies
  compassion, beauty, and abundance — heart-centered
  qualities of generosity and harmony.

Buddhism

- In Tibetan Buddhism, the **Green Tara** represents compassion in action, a quick-responding goddess who hears the cries of the world and answers immediately.
- **Avalokiteshvara (Chenrezig in Tibet, Kannon/Guanyin in East Asia)** is the Bodhisattva of Compassion, often shown with a thousand arms and eyes — symbolizing the heart's infinite capacity to see suffering and respond with love.

Sufism (Islamic Mysticism)

- In Sufi poetry, the **Beloved** (God) is said to dwell in the lover's heart. Rumi wrote: *"Your heart is the size of an ocean. Go find yourself in its hidden depths."*
- The Sufi practice of polishing the "mirror of the heart" parallels Anahata purification — making the heart clear enough to reflect divine beauty.

Kabbalah

- The sefirah **Tiferet** on the Tree of Life is often linked to the heart. Tiferet means "beauty" and represents balance, harmony, and the seat of divine compassion.
- It is sometimes personified as the union of masculine (Ze'ir Anpin) and feminine (Shekhinah) energies — echoing Ishvara and Kakini.

Indigenous & Earth-Based Traditions

- In many Native American teachings, the heart is honored as the center of **the Great Spirit's voice within us.** Elders teach that the heart is where we hear truth and guidance.

- In Andean cosmology, the **Chakana (Andean cross)** is linked to the heart as a center of balance between worlds.

The Universal Lesson

Across cultures, the deities and sacred figures of the heart remind us of the same truth: **the heart is the dwelling place of the divine.** Whether through Ishvara and Kakini, Krishna and Radha, Avalokiteshvara, Christ, or the Sufi Beloved, the message is the same — love is both our deepest essence and the gateway to the infinite.

THE ELEMENT OF ANAHATA: AIR (VĀYU)

Each chakra is traditionally aligned with one of the five great elements of nature (*pancha mahabhutas*). For the Heart Chakra, that element is **air — Vāyu** in Sanskrit. This is not an arbitrary link; it is a profound reflection of the qualities of the heart itself.

Air as the Language of the Heart

Air is movement. It is invisible, but we feel it on our skin, in the rustle of leaves, in the rise and fall of our chest with every breath. The heart, too, is unseen yet deeply felt. Just as air surrounds and connects everything on Earth, the heart connects us — to ourselves, to others, to all of life.

- **Breath as Life Force:** In yoga, the word *prana* means both "breath" and "life energy." Without breath, there is no life. Without love, there is no true living.
- **Freedom and Expansion:** Air cannot be contained. It flows freely, moving around and through everything. A balanced heart carries the same freedom — love that expands without clinging or controlling.

- **Lightness and Space:** Air gives us the feeling of openness, like a wide sky. When the heart is balanced, it feels spacious, light, and unburdened.

Why Air Belongs to the Heart

The lower chakras (earth, water, fire) are denser elements — they root us in the physical world. The higher chakras (ether/space and beyond) open us to spiritual dimensions. But **air, at the heart, is the bridge**. It is lighter than matter but denser than pure space, making it the perfect meeting point between body and spirit.

Air teaches the heart to:

- **Flow rather than force.**
- **Expand rather than constrict.**
- **Connect rather than isolate.**

Meditating on Air

Bringing the element of air into your heart practices can be simple yet profound:

1. **Breath Awareness:** Place your hand on your chest. Feel your inhale expand the ribs. Feel your exhale soften the chest. Whisper silently: *"I am open. I am free."*
2. **Wind Meditation:** Sit outdoors where the breeze can touch you. Imagine each gust is the breath of life itself, reminding you that you are never separate.
3. **Visualization:** Envision your chest filled with a glowing green sky. With each breath, this sky expands outward, limitless and clear.

Air in Daily Life

- **When the heart feels heavy:** Step outside. Breathe deeply. Let the wind carry away the weight.
- **When relationships feel tight or controlling:** Imagine more space — between breaths, between words, between hearts. Allow love to breathe.
- **When you need inspiration:** Remember that inspiration literally means "to breathe in." Open your heart to fresh air, and new ideas, perspectives, and connections flow in.

The Lesson of Air

Air reminds us that love is not meant to be held too tightly. Just as you cannot grasp the wind in your hand, you cannot lock love into a cage. It must flow, circulate, and move freely — within you and around you. A heart aligned with air becomes a vast sky: open, boundless, and full of life.

THE ANIMAL SYMBOL OF ANAHATA: ANTELOPE / BLACKBUCK

In the ancient chakra system, each energy center was given an animal guide — a living emblem that carried its essence into form. For the Heart Chakra, that animal is the **antelope (sometimes depicted specifically as the Indian blackbuck, a swift and elegant deer-like creature).**

Why the Antelope?

The antelope is known for its grace, lightness, and astonishing speed. When startled, it leaps effortlessly, bounding across the earth with an elegance that looks almost otherworldly. This imagery mirrors the qualities of the heart when it is open:

- **Lightness:** The antelope moves without heaviness, just as love frees us from the weight of fear and resentment.
- **Openness:** With wide, watchful eyes, it lives in constant awareness of its surroundings — a reminder that the heart, too, thrives when it is open and receptive.
- **Swiftness of Spirit:** Love can come upon us suddenly, like the quick leap of an antelope — a spark that changes everything in an instant.

SYMBOLISM IN THE HEART CHAKRA

The antelope represents:

- **Freedom:** A heart in balance does not cling; it moves with trust and agility.
- **Alertness:** Like the antelope that senses subtle shifts in its environment, the heart tuned to Anahata perceives the emotional atmosphere around it.
- **The Leap of Love:** The animal's bound is a metaphor for the heart's leap of faith — into trust, into relationship, into the unknown of vulnerability.

Meditating with the Antelope

- **Visualization:** Imagine a glowing green field in your chest, and see an antelope leaping freely within it. Each leap is a release of fear, a step deeper into joy.
- **Affirmation:** *"My heart is light. My love moves freely. I leap into life with trust."*
- **Nature Practice:** Watch deer or other wild animals if you can; notice their grace and awareness. Let that quality awaken in your own heart.

The Deeper Lesson

The antelope shows us that the heart was never meant to be caged. When wounded, the heart contracts — it grows heavy, guarded, reluctant. But when healed, it moves like the antelope: free, swift, alive.

The blackbuck's horns — long, spiraling upward — are also symbolic. They remind us that the heart's energy, while grounded in the body, always reaches toward the heavens.

THE HEART AS THE SACRED CAVE

In the oldest yogic texts, long before chakras were drawn as lotus wheels, the sages spoke of the **Hridaya Guha** — the cave of the heart. This was not a physical cave hidden in the mountains, but an inner sanctuary, a secret chamber deep within every human being.

The Cave Within

The Hridaya Guha was described as a space hidden behind ordinary awareness, so subtle that most people never enter it. Yogis taught that in meditation, if you follow your breath and awareness inward, past the noise of thoughts and emotions, you can find this cave.

Inside, they said, burns a **tiny flame of light** — eternal, untouched by sorrow, loss, or fear. No matter what happens in your life, this flame remains pure, steady, and unbroken. It is the essence of who you are: the Self, the soul, the indwelling divine.

Why the Heart?

Why place this inner cave in the heart and not the mind? Because the heart is not only an organ of feeling but the seat of being. Across cultures, people instinctively point to their chest — not their head — when speaking of truth, love, or soul. The yogis knew that within the heart lies the doorway to ultimate reality.

- **In Tantra:** the cave is the seat of Anahata, where unstruck sound resonates.
- **In Vedanta:** the Upanishads say, *"The Self, smaller than a grain of rice, resides in the cave of the heart, radiant and immortal."*
- **In Christian Mysticism:** saints wrote of the "inner chamber of the heart" where Christ consciousness resides.

The Heart Chakra as a Map

The Heart Chakra symbol — with its petals, triangles, and circle — is more than decoration. It is a **map to the cave.** Each layer represents a threshold, guiding the meditator inward. To move from the outer petals to the innermost star is to travel from the surface world of roles and identities into the hidden sanctuary where the eternal flame burns.

A Practice: Entering the Cave

1. Close your eyes. Place your hand on your chest.
2. Imagine a small doorway there, opening with your breath.
3. Step inward in your mind's eye, walking down into a hidden cave.
4. At the center, see a flame glowing steadily — small, yet illuminating everything.
5. Sit before this flame. Know that it is *you* — your truest self, untouched by pain.

The Deeper Lesson

The cave of the heart reminds us that the world may shake, the body may weaken, and emotions may storm — but there is a place within untouched by it all. To return to this cave is to return to truth. To live from this cave is to live in freedom, love, and authenticity.

THE WESTERN ADAPTATION

When the chakra system was introduced to the West in the late 19th and early 20th centuries, much of this original context was reshaped. Theosophists such as C.W. Leadbeater and Alice Bailey translated the chakra teachings into language that Western audiences could grasp, emphasizing their connection to health, psychology, and spiritual development.

Later, in the 20th century, psychologists like Carl Jung drew parallels between chakras and stages of individuation, while healers in the New Age movement expanded them into frameworks for emotional and physical healing.

Today, in Western Reiki and energy healing practices, the Heart Chakra is often taught as the center of love, compassion, and relationships — a concept true to its roots, though sometimes simplified. While ancient yogis used Anahata to meditate on divine sound and unity, modern practitioners often use it as a practical tool for **balancing emotions, supporting physical health, and cultivating compassion in daily life.**

The hidden history of Anahata shows us that this chakra is not new — it is part of a lineage of wisdom stretching back thousands of years. As we move forward in this book, we'll draw on both the **ancient roots** and the **modern practices** to create a fuller, richer understanding of the heart's energy.

WANT TO SEE IT IN ACTION?...
Watch this video for more insight and tips on Chakras.

Watch it here: Chakras https://youtu.be/QcQTXV1dEJQ

Archetypes of the Heart Chakra

Every chakra expresses itself through patterns of behavior, belief, and energy. These patterns are often described as **archetypes** — timeless roles that live within us all. By exploring the archetypes of Anahata, we can better understand how the heart opens, closes, wounds, and heals.

WHY ARCHETYPES MATTER

Archetypes are like mirrors of the soul. They are patterns that have lived in humanity for thousands of years — universal ways of experiencing love, longing, wounding, and healing. In the Heart Chakra, archetypes give form to energies we often *feel* but cannot quite name.

Think of them as masks the heart wears to help us learn its lessons. Sometimes the mask is light-filled, showing us love's beauty. Other times, it slips into shadow, revealing where we have strayed from balance. By recognizing these archetypes in ourselves and others, we gain language and insight for the deeper patterns playing out in relationships and healing work.

HOW ARCHETYPES HELP YOU WORK WITH ANAHATA

- **Self-Discovery:** When you notice, *"Ah, I am in my Wounded Child right now,"* it shifts you from being *lost in the pattern* to *witnessing it with awareness.* Awareness itself begins the healing.
- **Compassion for Shadows:** Archetypes show that shadows are not failures — they are distortions of love searching for balance. Instead of judging jealousy, codependency, or emotional walls, you can see them as signals pointing toward growth.

- **Choice and Empowerment:** Every archetype carries both shadow and light. By naming the pattern, you can consciously step into its higher expression. For example, the Martyr can become the Compassionate Healer when boundaries and self-love are restored.

THE GIFT OF ARCHETYPES IN PRACTICE

For practitioners, archetypes become a diagnostic and healing tool. When a client struggles with self-love, you may recognize the Wounded Child archetype. When someone overgives until they collapse, the Martyr may be at play. By naming the pattern, you bring it out of the shadows, where it can finally be healed.

For individuals, archetypes invite you to see your own heart with gentleness. Instead of saying, *"I am broken,"* you begin to see, *"I am in a season of the Lover, learning balance,"* or *"My Healer is awakening."* This reframes struggle as part of the heart's mythic journey.

Living Archetypally

Ultimately, working with archetypes in the Heart Chakra is about wholeness. You are not just one archetype — you are all of them, woven together like threads of a tapestry. At different times in life, one may dominate, and another may fade into the background. The key is not to eliminate the shadow, but to integrate it — letting every facet of the heart serve love more deeply.

THE LOVER ARCHETYPE
Essence: Connection, Passion, Joy

The Lover is the part of the heart that longs for union — with people, with beauty, with life itself. When this archetype is alive in you, the world feels more vibrant. Colors are richer, music is sweeter, and relationships feel like sacred portals to something greater. The Lover does not just want to live — they want to *fall in love with living.*

Light Side of the Lover

In its balanced expression, the Lover brings warmth, delight, and intimacy:

- **Celebration of Intimacy:** Whether romantic or platonic, relationships become opportunities for deep presence and affection.
- **Appreciation of Beauty:** Art, music, poetry, and nature stir your soul. You see beauty everywhere, and your heart responds with joy.
- **Embodied Joy:** The Lover teaches you to savor — a touch, a laugh, a sunset. Life is not something to rush through but to drink deeply.
- **Generosity of Spirit:** Love flows outward easily. You naturally uplift others with affection and delight in connection.

When the Lover is awake, the heart feels like a flame that warms without burning, lighting up everything around it.

Shadow Side of the Lover

When unbalanced, the Lover's desire for passion can become distorted:

- **Addiction to Intensity:** The Lover may crave the thrill of romance or novelty, mistaking drama for love.
- **Fear of Loneliness:** This can lead to clinging, jealousy, or an inability to be alone.
- **Over-Identification with Others:** The Lover may lose their center, merging so much with another that they forget themselves.

- **Emotional Rollercoasters:** Relationships may feel euphoric one moment and devastating the next, as stability is sacrificed for intensity.

In shadow, the Lover forgets that the deepest union is within — and looks outside for what can only be rooted in the self.

Healing Practices for the Lover

Balancing this archetype is not about dimming passion, but anchoring it in a stable, loving foundation:

- **Self-Love First:** Spend time nurturing your own heart. Affirm: *"I am worthy of love, even when alone."*
- **Balance Passion with Presence:** Instead of chasing intensity, practice savoring simple moments — a breath, a flower, a song.
- **Sacred Solitude:** Learn to enjoy your own company. Solitude strengthens your capacity to love without clinging.
- **Grounded Sensuality:** Connect with the body through yoga, dance, or mindful touch, so love is rooted in the present rather than fantasy.
- **Heart-Centered Journaling Prompt:** *When do I mistake intensity for love? What small moments of beauty can I savor today?*

The Gift of the Lover

When healed and balanced, the Lover reminds us that the heart is meant to delight in connection. Love is not only a bond between people, but a way of being in relationship with all of life. The Lover teaches us to live with passion, to celebrate beauty, and to open fully to the joy of existence — without losing ourselves in the process.

THE HEALER ARCHETYPE
Essence: Compassion, Service, Nurturing

The Healer is the heart's instinct to mend, soothe, and bring wholeness. When this archetype is alive in you, you feel called to relieve suffering, to comfort others, and to radiate kindness into the world. The Healer embodies the truth that love is not just felt — it is given as a gift of presence.

Light Side of the Healer

In its balanced form, the Healer brings peace and renewal wherever they go:

- **Compassionate Presence:** Simply being with others creates safety. People often say, *"I feel better just talking to you."*
- **Natural Caregiving:** The Healer gravitates toward roles of service — counselor, teacher, nurse, energy worker, or simply the friend everyone turns to.
- **Forgiveness and Kindness:** The Healer carries a nonjudgmental heart, able to see beyond mistakes to the soul beneath.
- **Restorative Energy:** In Reiki, massage, or simply a hug, the Healer channels soothing energy that helps others realign.

Balanced Healers remember that their greatest tool is not technique, but the love flowing through their heart.

Shadow Side of the Healer

When unbalanced, the Healer's gifts can turn heavy:

- **Overgiving:** Always caring for others while neglecting self-care.

- **Taking On Pain:** Absorbing others' emotions or illnesses until they feel drained or unwell themselves.
- **Martyrdom:** Sacrificing so much for others that resentment builds.
- **Attachment to "Fixing":** Believing healing is their responsibility, rather than allowing divine energy to flow through.

In shadow, the Healer forgets that they are a *channel*, not the source, of healing.

Healing Practices for the Healer

To restore balance, the Healer must learn to care for themselves as much as they care for others:

- **Set Boundaries with Love:** Practice saying, *"I can hold space for you, but I cannot carry this for you."*
- **Self-Nourishment Rituals:** Prioritize rest, healthy food, meditation, and time in nature. Fill your own cup first.
- **Energy Hygiene:** After sessions, clear your energy field with Reiki, breathwork, or visualization. Release what is not yours.
- **Shift Perspective:** Remember: healing does not come *from* you, but *through* you. You are the channel, not the source.
- **Heart-Centered Journaling Prompt:** *Where in my life am I giving too much? What would it look like to receive with the same openness I give?*

The Gift of the Healer

When balanced, the Healer radiates love without depletion. They embody compassion while remaining rooted, showing others that healing is not about fixing but about remembering wholeness. Their presence reminds us that true healing is an act of love — and that love begins by including ourselves in its embrace.

THE WOUNDED CHILD ARCHETYPE
Essence: Innocence, Vulnerability, Unmet Needs

The Wounded Child is the part of the heart that remembers pain from the past — moments when love felt absent, unsafe, or conditional. It carries the raw tenderness of early experiences, where rejection, abandonment, or neglect left imprints. Yet within this archetype also lives innocence, creativity, and play — qualities that can blossom again when the child within feels safe and seen.

Light Side of the Wounded Child

When nurtured and acknowledged, this archetype becomes a source of tenderness and authenticity:

- **Awakened Innocence:** A natural sense of wonder and play re-emerges. Life feels less guarded, more curious.
- **Creativity and Imagination:** The Wounded Child often holds hidden gifts of artistic expression, storytelling, or playfulness.
- **Empathy and Gentleness:** Having known pain, the healed Child develops deep compassion for others.
- **Authenticity:** The healed Child is unafraid to be vulnerable, modeling the courage it takes to live with an open heart.

Balanced, the Wounded Child reminds us that love is not earned — it is our birthright.

Shadow Side of the Wounded Child

When unhealed, this archetype continues to replay old patterns of pain:

- **Emotional Walls:** Hiding behind defenses, refusing to risk closeness.
- **Fear of Intimacy:** Longing for connection but retreating when it feels too vulnerable.
- **Repeating Old Wounds:** Seeking love in unsafe places, recreating dynamics of rejection or neglect.
- **Need for Validation:** Constantly looking outside for reassurance of worthiness.

In shadow, the Wounded Child believes, *"If they really knew me, they wouldn't stay."* This belief silently sabotages love.

Healing Practices for the Wounded Child

Healing this archetype requires tenderness and consistency, as if re-parenting the inner self:

- **Inner Child Work:** Visualize yourself holding the younger you, offering comfort, love, and safety.
- **Self-Compassion:** Speak to yourself with kindness, as you would to a child who is hurting.
- **Re-Parenting Rituals:** Give yourself what was missing — play, creativity, nurturing routines, or simple permission to feel.
- **Affirmations:** Repeat: *"You are safe. You are loved. You belong."*
- **Heart-Centered Journaling Prompt:** *What did my younger self most need to hear? How can I give that to myself now?*

The Gift of the Wounded Child

When embraced, the Wounded Child becomes a teacher of resilience and tenderness. It shows us that vulnerability is not weakness but a doorway to deeper love. By holding the child within with compassion, we learn to hold others with greater

care. The gift of this archetype is the rediscovery of innocence
— a heart that trusts again, plays again, and loves again.

THE MARTYR ARCHETYPE
Essence: Sacrifice, Endurance, Loyalty

The Martyr is the part of the heart that knows how to endure
and give for the sake of others. It represents devotion, loyalty,
and the willingness to put personal desires aside in the service
of love or a higher cause. At its core, the Martyr archetype
reveals the heart's capacity to commit fully — even at great
cost.

Light Side of the Martyr

When balanced, the Martyr becomes a source of strength and
inspiration:

- **Devotion:** Offers steadfast love, loyalty, and service to
  people, communities, or spiritual callings.
- **Selflessness:** Places the needs of others above personal
  comfort when it truly matters, embodying compassion in
  action.
- **Resilience:** Demonstrates endurance through challenges,
  inspiring others by example.
- **Sacred Service:** Gives from a place of love and choice,
  not duty, creating genuine impact.

In its light, the Martyr reminds us that love sometimes requires
sacrifice — not as a burden, but as a conscious gift of the heart.

Shadow Side of the Martyr

When distorted, the Martyr archetype confuses love with
suffering and sacrifice:

- **Neglect of Self:** Consistently puts others' needs ahead of their own, leading to exhaustion or illness.
- **Suppressed Emotions:** Silences anger, sadness, or desire, believing they must "be strong" for others.
- **Unspoken Expectations:** Gives without boundaries, then carries resentment when love is not returned.
- **Suffering as Identity:** Equates pain with devotion, believing that enduring hardship proves worth or love.

In shadow, the Martyr's sacrifice is no longer sacred — it becomes a silent chain of obligation.

Healing Practices for the Martyr

To rebalance this archetype, the Martyr must shift from unconscious sacrifice to empowered choice:

- **Sacred Choice:** Reframe giving as a choice, not a duty. Ask: *"Am I giving from love, or from fear of rejection?"*
- **Boundaries Without Guilt:** Practice saying *"no"* as an act of self-love, not selfishness.
- **Release Resentment:** Journal or meditate on places where unspoken expectations have built walls.
- **Redefine Devotion:** Learn that love is not proven by suffering, but by joy and presence.
- **Heart-Centered Journaling Prompt:** *Where in my life do I give past my limits? How can I serve in ways that nourish both others and myself?*

The Gift of the Martyr

When healed, the Martyr becomes a beacon of sacred service. Instead of collapsing under obligation, they choose service as an expression of love. Their endurance becomes resilience, their loyalty becomes devotion, and their sacrifice becomes freedom. The Martyr teaches that true love is not about losing yourself for others, but about finding yourself more fully as you serve from the heart.

Heart Archetype Reflection Exercise

Take some quiet time with a journal, or simply close your eyes and reflect. Read each archetype and ask yourself the questions that follow. There are no right or wrong answers — only insights into how your heart is expressing itself right now.

THE LOVER

- When do I feel most alive, passionate, and connected?
- Do I sometimes chase intensity instead of stability in love or relationships?
- How can I bring more grounded joy into my life without losing the spark?

THE HEALER

- In what ways do I naturally bring comfort and compassion to others?
- Where might I be giving too much, leaving myself depleted?
- What boundary could I set that would make my love more sustainable?

THE WOUNDED CHILD

- What old hurt still lingers in my heart?
- How does my inner child show up when I feel scared or unloved?
- What could I say or do today to reassure that part of me that it is safe and loved?

THE MARTYR

- Where in my life do I sacrifice my needs for others?
- Do I carry unspoken resentment when I give too much?
- How could I transform sacrifice into conscious, joyful choice?

INTEGRATION PROMPT

- Which archetype feels most alive in me right now?
- Which archetype needs the most healing or balancing?
- What small action could I take this week to live from the *light side* of that archetype?

Chapter 3 – The Energetic Blueprint of the Heart

The Heart Chakra and the Aura

Every chakra doesn't just spin within the body; it also radiates outward into the **aura**, the field of energy that surrounds and permeates you. Think of the aura as your energetic atmosphere — invisible to most eyes, but constantly shifting in response to your health, emotions, and spiritual state.

The Heart Chakra is most closely connected to the fourth layer of the aura, also known as the **astral layer**. This layer is where the emotional and spiritual aspects of love meet, shaping how you bond with yourself, others, and the greater web of life.

When the Heart Chakra is balanced, the fourth layer of the aura appears **vibrant and clear**, often glowing with shades of green, rose, or gold. This radiance reflects compassion, emotional openness, and the ability to give and receive love without fear. Sensitive practitioners may perceive it as a warm field that draws people in with a sense of safety and trust.

When the Heart Chakra is blocked or imbalanced, the aura in this layer can appear **muddy, collapsed, or jagged**. The green light may turn dull, or streaks of gray and red may ripple through the field. This reflects unresolved grief, anger, jealousy, or fear of intimacy. Instead of radiating warmth, the aura feels withdrawn, protective, or even prickly to others.

The fourth aura layer is also where many **energetic cords** are
formed — subtle connections between your heart and the hearts
of others. These cords can be healthy and life-giving, such as
the loving bond between parent and child, or draining and
restrictive, as in toxic or co-dependent relationships.
Practitioners working with the Heart Chakra often sense, clear,
or heal these cords to restore balance in both people's energy
fields.

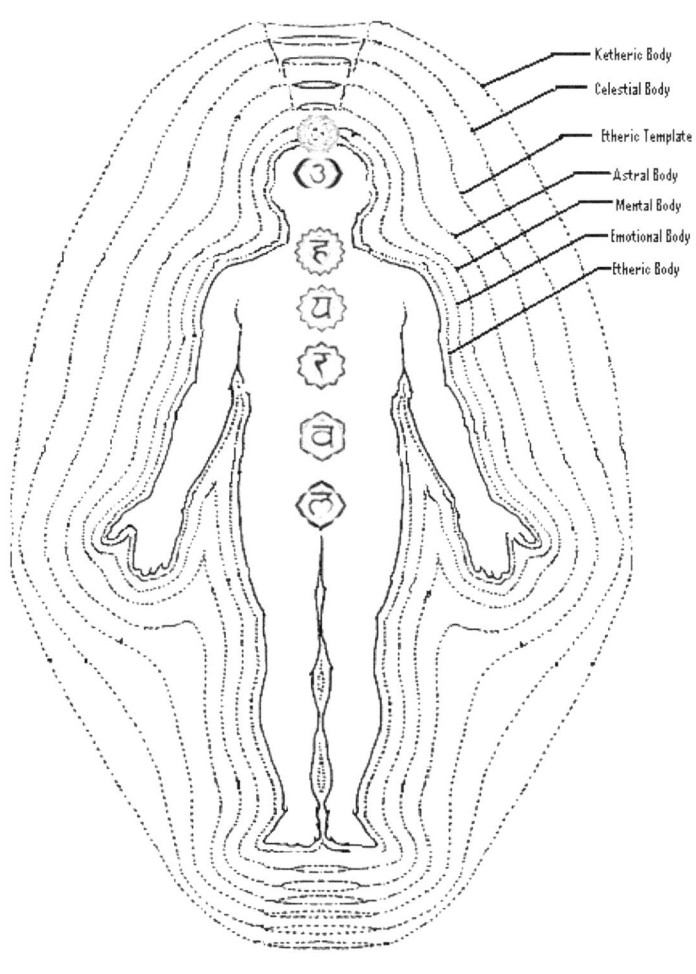

THE AURA AS YOUR PERSONAL ENERGY FIELD

Just as the Earth has a magnetic field that surrounds and protects it, your body also has an energetic field — the **aura**. The Earth's field is invisible, yet it affects everything from compass needles to the movement of solar winds. In the same way, your aura is not usually seen with the eyes, but it influences how energy flows within you and how you interact with the world around you.

The Heart Chakra plays a central role in this personal field. Its energy radiates outward into the **fourth layer of the aura**, shaping the "climate" of your emotional and spiritual environment. When Anahata is balanced, your aura resembles a clear and strong magnetic field — harmonious, radiant, and resilient. When imbalanced, it can look more like a stormy atmosphere, turbulent or weakened, leaving you vulnerable to emotional strain or external stress.

Thinking of the aura like the Earth's field helps us understand why maintaining balance in the Heart Chakra is so important. Just as disturbances in the Earth's field can affect weather and communication systems, disturbances in your aura can ripple through your relationships, emotions, and even physical health.

By keeping your Heart Chakra open and balanced, you help your energetic field remain stable, allowing you to live with greater harmony, clarity, and connection.

WHY THE AURA CONNECTION MATTERS

Understanding the Heart Chakra's link to the aura helps practitioners in two ways:

1. **Personal Awareness**
   - You begin to notice how your emotions ripple outward. Love, gratitude, and forgiveness

expand the aura. Resentment, fear, or grief can constrict it.

2. **Healing Practice**
   - o During Reiki or energy work, you may feel differences in the field above the chest. Tingling, warmth, or resistance are all signs of how the aura is reflecting the state of the Heart Chakra.
   - o Balancing the chakra not only restores internal harmony but also **re-patterns the aura**, making your entire energy field more resilient and radiant.

WANT TO SEE IT IN ACTION?...

Watch this video for more insight and tips on Auras.

Watch it here: Seeing an Aura https://youtu.be/uGEjO3-7EHA and https://youtu.be/KM-JdQCZ2Gw

The Flow of Energy Through the Heart Chakra

The Heart Chakra is often called the **bridge chakra**, because it sits at the center of your energy system. Even if you don't yet know much about the other chakras, you can imagine the heart as the **crossroads** where all energies meet.

Energy from the lower body — the grounding forces of survival, stability, creativity, and personal power — rises upward. Energy from the upper body — the realms of expression, intuition, and connection to the divine — flows downward. The two currents meet in the heart.

This makes the Heart Chakra the **balancing point**. It blends earth with sky, physical life with inner awareness, and human experience with higher purpose. When your heart energy is open and balanced, energy flows smoothly in both directions, like a well-functioning bridge that allows traffic to move freely.

But when the Heart Chakra is blocked, that flow is disrupted. Energy may feel stuck in the lower centers — leaving you focused only on survival, control, or old wounds. Or it may rush upward without grounding — leaving you scattered, unbalanced, or disconnected from daily life. In either case, harmony is lost until the heart reopens.

This is why healers say the heart is the **true center of integration**. It is the place where love and compassion create balance between all other aspects of your being. By tending to the heart, you don't just heal one chakra — you help the **entire system** flow in harmony.

The Heart as the Seat of the Soul

Across traditions and throughout history, the heart has been regarded as more than a physical organ. It has been honored as the **dwelling place of the soul** — the place where life, love, and spirit meet. This universal idea reminds us that the heart is not just part of the body, but the center of who we are.

HINDU & YOGIC TRADITIONS

In yogic and Tantric philosophy, the heart (Anahata) is considered the **gateway to the higher self.** It is said to be the place where *Atman* (the individual soul) resides in union with *Brahman* (the universal soul). Yogis often meditated on the heart center to experience the quiet sound of the soul — the *"unstruck sound"* of Anahata — and to feel the presence of eternal consciousness within.

TIBETAN BUDDHISM

Tibetan texts describe the heart center as the place where the **"indestructible drop"** of clear light consciousness is found. Even at the moment of death, when the winds and elements dissolve, this indestructible essence at the heart remains. It is said to carry the continuity of the soul into future lives.

ANCIENT EGYPTIAN TRADITION

For the Egyptians, the heart was considered the **seat of the soul and conscience.** In the afterlife, a person's heart was weighed against the feather of Ma'at (truth and justice). If the heart was pure and balanced, the soul could move on. This shows how the heart was seen as the measure of one's spiritual essence.

CHRISTIAN MYSTICISM

In Christianity, mystics speak of the heart as the **inner dwelling place of Christ**. The devotion to the *Sacred Heart of Jesus* symbolizes divine love radiating from within the human heart. Many saints taught that to pray with the heart was to meet God at the very center of the soul, where love and grace reside.

SUFI (ISLAMIC MYSTICISM)

In Sufi teachings, the heart (*qalb*) is the **spiritual center of being.** It is where divine love is received and where the seeker experiences closeness to God. The polished heart reflects divine truth like a mirror; when clouded by ego or worldly attachments, it cannot reflect the light of the soul.

WESTERN PHILOSOPHY

Even in ancient Greece, philosophers such as Aristotle considered the heart to be the center of thought, emotion, and life force. Long before the brain was understood, the heart was seen as the **seat of consciousness.**

A Universal Understanding

Though the words differ — *Atman, soul, spirit, conscience, divine spark* — the teaching is the same: the heart is more than flesh and blood. It is the **seat of the soul**, the place where your truest essence lives.

For those working with the Heart Chakra, this understanding gives profound meaning to healing. When you open Anahata, you are not only balancing energy; you are awakening the soul's own dwelling place, allowing your deepest truth to shine through.

How Practitioners Work with the Heart Chakra

Different healing traditions and modalities approach the Heart Chakra in unique ways, but the essence is the same: opening, sensing, and balancing the flow of energy through Anahata to restore harmony.

WHAT "FLOW OF ENERGY THROUGH ANAHATA" MEANS

1. **The Heart as a Bridge**
   Anahata sits in the center of the chakra system. The three lower chakras carry grounding, survival, sexuality, and personal power. The three upper chakras carry communication, intuition, and spiritual awareness.
   - Energy rises **upward** from the lower chakras toward the heart.
   - Energy descends **downward** from the higher chakras toward the heart.
   - In the heart, the two currents meet, blend, and balance.

2. **The Circulation of Life Force**
   In many traditions (yogic *prana*, Chinese *qi*, Japanese *ki*), life force is constantly circulating through the body. The Heart Chakra filters and transforms this flow. When it is balanced, energy moves smoothly through the chest and radiates outward into the aura, especially the fourth layer (the astral field of love and connection).

3. **The Exchange Between Inner and Outer Worlds**
   The "flow" also refers to how the Heart Chakra manages the **give-and-receive cycle of love**.
   - If energy flows outward freely, you can express love, compassion, and kindness.
   - If energy flows inward freely, you can accept love, care, and connection from others.

○ When this cycle is blocked, people often either overgive (losing themselves) or block receiving (closing off emotionally).

4. **Movement Within the Chakra Itself**
   Each chakra is described as a spinning wheel. Energy enters from both the **front** (chest/sternum) and the **back** (between the shoulder blades). "Flow" means the chakra is rotating smoothly, drawing in life force, and releasing it in balance. If it's blocked, the wheel feels sluggish; if it's overactive, it can feel chaotic or overwhelming.

Basically: *"flow of energy through Anahata,"* is referring to all of these together:

- **Vertical flow** between lower and higher chakras.
- **Circulating life force** through the chest and aura.
- **Relational flow** of giving and receiving love.
- **Chakra rotation** itself, the wheel spinning in balance.

REIKI PRACTITIONERS

In Reiki, practitioners often begin by **scanning the energy field** with their hands a few inches above the chest. Many report feeling warmth, tingling, or subtle pulsing where the heart's energy is active. If the chakra feels heavy or blocked, the practitioner may sense resistance, coolness, or irregular flow.

To activate and balance the Heart Chakra, Reiki practitioners place their hands gently over the sternum or between the shoulder blades. Energy is channeled not only through technique but through **intention and compassion**. A clear and open heart in the practitioner allows healing energy to flow freely to the client, often leaving both feeling calmer, lighter, and more connected.

ENERGY HEALERS & INTUITIVES

Some energy healers and intuitive practitioners sense heart energy through **visual impressions** or inner knowing rather than touch. They may see colors in the aura — vibrant green or pink for balance, dull or muddy tones when blocked. Others describe emotional impressions, such as sudden waves of grief, joy, or compassion that reflect the client's heart state.

These practitioners may activate the Heart Chakra using visualization, sound healing (such as toning the seed sound *YAM*), or by guiding clients through meditations that release grief and open space for love.

ACUPUNCTURISTS & TRADITIONAL CHINESE MEDICINE

In Chinese Medicine, practitioners focus on the **Heart and Lung meridians**, which mirror many of Anahata's qualities. Palpating pulse points, examining the tongue, or observing the complexion may reveal imbalances in the heart's energy. Treatment might involve placing needles along heart or lung points, using herbs to calm the spirit (*shen*), or breath practices to strengthen the lungs. Though the language differs, the goal is the same: restoring joy, openness, and flow in the heart.

SOMATIC & BODY-ORIENTED PRACTITIONERS

Massage therapists, breathwork facilitators, and somatic healers often notice that the chest and shoulders carry emotional tension linked to the Heart Chakra. Tight muscles, shallow breathing, or protective postures can signal blocked energy. By opening the chest through touch, guided breath, or movement, these practitioners help release old emotions, allowing the heart to expand.

MYSTICAL & SPIRITUAL TRADITIONS

Mystics, shamans, and spiritual teachers may approach the heart as the **dwelling place of the soul**. Practices include chanting, prayer, or rituals that honor the heart as a sacred center. For them, activating heart energy is less about "fixing" and more about **awakening the remembrance of love** as our natural state.

A COMMON THREAD

No matter the modality — Reiki, energy healing, acupuncture, bodywork, or prayer — practitioners agree on one truth: the heart is a **gateway to transformation**. When its energy is open and flowing, healing happens naturally. When it is blocked, no amount of technique can fully restore balance until love is present.

Chapter 4 – Signs of Imbalance

Shadow Aspects of the Heart Chakra

While the Heart Chakra is the home of love, compassion, and connection, it can also express its shadow. These shadows aren't signs of failure — they are invitations to see where love has been twisted by fear, unmet needs, or unhealed wounds. By naming them, we create the possibility of healing.

CODEPENDENCY: LOVE ENTANGLED

- **What it is:** Codependency happens when your sense of worth is tied to being needed by others. Instead of love flowing freely, it becomes a bargain: "If I take care of you, will you love me?"
- **How it feels inside:** Anxiety when alone, fear of rejection, difficulty knowing who you are without the relationship.
- **How it looks outwardly:** Over-giving, rescuing, or sacrificing to the point of depletion.
- **Healing path:** Strengthen boundaries, cultivate self-love, and remember: true connection comes from wholeness, not dependence.

EMOTIONAL MANIPULATION: LOVE DISTORTED

- **What it is:** When the heart is wounded, love can become a tool to control rather than connect. Emotional manipulation can appear as guilt-tripping, silent treatment, or exaggerated displays of need.
- **How it feels inside:** Fear of abandonment, insecurity, or a belief that honesty won't get you the love you need.
- **How it looks outwardly:** Using guilt, pity, or pressure to pull others closer.
- **Healing path:** Practice vulnerability. Replace manipulation with honest expression: *"I feel hurt and need support"* instead of subtle control.

NARCISSISTIC WOUNDS: LOVE GUARDED

- **What it is:** At its core, narcissism is not too much love of self, but *too little.* A wounded heart builds defenses of arrogance, entitlement, or superiority to protect deep insecurity.
- **How it feels inside:** Hidden shame, fear of being unworthy, or emptiness beneath the surface of confidence.
- **How it looks outwardly:** Demanding admiration, difficulty with empathy, or dismissing others' needs.
- **Healing path:** Gradual softening through safe love, practicing empathy, and learning to receive without fear of losing control.

THE INVITATION OF SHADOW WORK

Shadow aspects of the heart don't mean love is gone — only that it has been clouded by pain. When we bring awareness, compassion, and healing to these shadows, they transform:

- Codependency becomes interdependence.
- Manipulation becomes honest expression.

- Narcissistic wounds become authentic self-love.

The shadow is not the opposite of love; it is love calling out to be healed.

SHADOW-TO-LIGHT TRANSFORMATION: HEART CHAKRA

Shadow Expression	How It Shows Up	Balanced / Light Expression	Healing Path
Codependency	Over-giving, rescuing, identity tied to being needed	Interdependence – healthy balance of giving and receiving	Build self-worth, set loving boundaries, practice self-care
Emotional Manipulation	Guilt-tripping, silent treatment, indirect control	Authentic Communication – honest, vulnerable sharing of needs	Practice direct expression, develop emotional awareness, release fear of rejection
Narcissistic Wounds	Entitlement, superiority, lack of empathy masking deep insecurity	Authentic Self-Love & Empathy – honoring self without diminishing others	Inner child healing, safe relationships, practicing compassion
Jealousy	Suspicion, fear of being	Trust & Security in Love	Grounding practices, self-love

Shadow Expression	How It Shows Up	Balanced / Light Expression	Healing Path
	replaced, comparison	– confidence in self and partner	rituals, affirmations of worth
Clinginess	Over-dependence, fear of abandonment, constant reassurance seeking	Secure Attachment – closeness without fear	Develop independence, build confidence, learn to enjoy solitude
Isolation	Emotional walls, avoidance of closeness, loneliness	Healthy Solitude & Openness – choosing connection without fear	Inner healing of grief, forgiveness practices, gentle social connection

HOW TO USE THIS TABLE

- **Practitioners:** Keep it as a quick diagnostic tool — notice shadow patterns in clients and guide them toward the light side.
- **Readers:** Journal about which shadow shows up most often in your own life, and commit to one healing practice to begin shifting it.

Blocked or Deficient Heart Energy

When the Heart Chakra is blocked or deficient, the natural flow of love, compassion, and connection becomes restricted. Instead of radiating warmth, the energy of the heart feels contracted, guarded, or absent. This imbalance often arises from unresolved grief, past betrayal, or fear of being hurt again.

Isolation: When the Heart Pulls Away

One of the clearest signs of a blocked or deficient Heart Chakra is **isolation**. This isn't the nourishing kind of solitude that restores your spirit — it is the protective kind, born out of fear or past wounds. The heart pulls away from others in an attempt to stay safe, but in doing so, it also shuts itself off from love, connection, and healing.

WHY IT HAPPENS

Isolation often grows out of experiences where love felt unsafe. A painful breakup, betrayal, rejection, or early childhood neglect can teach the heart to hide. Instead of risking being hurt again, the energy of Anahata contracts, building invisible walls to keep others out. On the surface, these walls may look like independence, strength, or self-protection. But underneath lies fear — fear of being vulnerable, of being let down, or of not being enough.

HOW IT FEELS INSIDE

- A persistent sense of loneliness, even when surrounded by people.
- A hollow or empty feeling in the chest, as if something vital is missing.
- Difficulty trusting others with your true thoughts and feelings.
- A longing for closeness paired with an equally strong fear of letting anyone in.
- Feeling like an outsider, disconnected from the "flow" of life.

This inner experience is often confusing. The heart craves connection but resists it at the same time, leaving you stuck in a cycle of yearning and withdrawal.

HOW IT APPEARS OUTWARDLY

- You may avoid deep conversations, steering interactions toward small talk or practical matters.
- You might keep relationships surface-level, never letting others get close enough to see the real you.
- Friends or loved ones may describe you as distant, guarded, or hard to read.
- Body language often reflects the block: crossed arms, hunched shoulders, or avoiding eye contact.
- In some cases, you may isolate physically — spending long periods alone, avoiding social gatherings, or cutting ties when relationships feel too vulnerable.

THE COST OF ISOLATION

At first, these walls may feel protective, but over time, they become prisons. Isolation may prevent pain, but it also prevents joy, intimacy, and healing. A blocked Heart Chakra leaves you watching life from the sidelines instead of participating fully. Over years, this can manifest not only as emotional emptiness, but also as physical symptoms in the chest — tightness, shallow breathing, or weakened immunity.

THE HIDDEN TRUTH

What isolation really shows is not the absence of love, but the **fear of losing love.** The heart longs to connect, but past wounds convince it that safety comes from withdrawal. Recognizing this is the first step toward healing — understanding that the walls built to protect the heart may also be the very walls keeping love away.

Bitterness: When the Heart Hardens

Another sign of a blocked or deficient Heart Chakra is **bitterness**. Where isolation builds walls, bitterness builds armor — a tough, protective shell that keeps others from getting too close. This isn't who you truly are, but rather what happens when the heart carries the weight of old wounds without release. Instead of softening through forgiveness, the heart becomes rigid, locked in resentment or cynicism.

WHY IT HAPPENS

Bitterness is often born out of deep disappointment. Maybe love wasn't returned, a betrayal cut too deeply, or repeated losses left scars. Over time, the mind replays these wounds like an old recording, and the heart responds by closing its doors. The belief becomes: *"If I don't expect love, I can't be hurt by it again."*

This may feel protective, but bitterness doesn't shield the heart — it traps it. By holding onto past pain, you carry it into every new experience, never allowing love to show up fresh.

HOW IT FEELS INSIDE

- A heaviness in the chest, as though carrying unresolved anger.
- Replaying betrayals or disappointments in your mind long after they happened.
- Struggling to let go of grudges, even when you want to.
- Distrust when love or kindness is offered — waiting for the "catch."
- A sense that love is unsafe, unreliable, or always conditional.

This inner bitterness often hides sadness beneath it. Anger feels easier to carry than grief, but both weigh down the heart when left unresolved.

HOW IT APPEARS OUTWARDLY

- Using sarcasm or sharp humor to deflect vulnerability.
- Criticizing others to avoid acknowledging your own pain.
- Meeting kindness or closeness with skepticism or dismissal.
- Shutting down emotionally when people try to connect, creating distance without explanation.
- Being described as "cold," "hard," or "guarded," even if you secretly long for closeness.

THE COST OF BITTERNESS

Bitterness slowly erodes trust, making genuine connections harder and harder. Relationships may become tense or surface-level, as others sense the walls of resentment. Physically, bitterness can manifest as tightness in the chest, chronic tension in the shoulders, or even heart-related health issues. Spiritually, it blocks the flow of compassion and prevents the soul from resting in love.

THE HIDDEN TRUTH

Beneath bitterness lies a tender truth: the heart has been hurt and doesn't know how to release the pain. The hardness is a disguise for vulnerability, a way of saying, *"I don't want to be hurt again."* Recognizing this doesn't mean ignoring betrayal or pretending everything is fine — it means acknowledging the wound with compassion so the heart can soften again.

Fear of Intimacy: Longing for Love, Yet Pulling Away

Perhaps the most painful expression of a blocked Heart Chakra is **fear of intimacy**. Unlike isolation or bitterness, which keep others at a distance outright, this imbalance is marked by an inner conflict — the desire for closeness battling against the fear of being hurt. The result is a push-pull dynamic: you long for love, yet retreat as soon as it begins to unfold.

WHY IT HAPPENS

Fear of intimacy often stems from past wounds of rejection, abandonment, or betrayal. If love once meant loss or pain, the heart learns to associate vulnerability with danger. The subconscious message becomes: *"If I let someone see me fully, they will leave, or they will hurt me."*

This fear isn't a lack of love — it's the **overprotection of love.** The heart craves connection so deeply that it tries to shield itself from the very risk that makes intimacy possible.

HOW IT FEELS INSIDE

- A constant tension between craving closeness and fearing it.
- Anxiety about being "too much" or "not enough" for someone to truly love.
- Difficulty relaxing into vulnerability — always scanning for signs of rejection.
- A tendency to overanalyze interactions, replaying conversations to see if you revealed "too much."
- A nagging fear that if people saw the real you, they would not stay.

This internal conflict often creates exhaustion, as the heart swings between hope and fear, openness and withdrawal.

HOW IT APPEARS OUTWARDLY

- Sabotaging relationships just when they begin to deepen, often without fully realizing why.
- Avoiding commitment by keeping relationships casual, distant, or short-lived.
- Pretending not to need anyone, hiding vulnerability behind independence or busyness.
- Pulling away emotionally or physically when someone offers real closeness.
- Choosing partners who are unavailable or distant, unconsciously mirroring your own fear of intimacy.

THE COST OF FEAR OF INTIMACY

This fear creates a cycle of loneliness. You may push others away while secretly longing for them to break through your walls. The heart feels caught in limbo — never fully alone, but never fully connected. Over time, this tension can manifest physically as tightness in the chest, shallow breathing, or nervous energy in the body.

THE HIDDEN TRUTH

Beneath the fear lies a very human longing: to be seen, known, and loved exactly as you are. The fear is not proof that you're unworthy of love — it is proof of how much you value love and how deeply you wish to protect your heart. Recognizing this truth allows the healing journey to begin, because the first step is not to force intimacy, but to meet your own fear with compassion.

WHY THIS MATTERS

A blocked or deficient Heart Chakra doesn't just limit relationships — it affects your entire well-being. The chest may feel tight, breathing shallow, and emotions heavy. Spiritually, you may feel cut off from love itself, unsure how to connect with God, Source, or the greater web of life.

The good news is that these blocks are not permanent. The heart is resilient. With awareness, compassion, and practice, even the most guarded heart can soften and return to its natural rhythm of love and openness.

Excess or Overactive Heart Energy

While a blocked heart hides behind walls, an overactive heart overflows without balance. Love and connection are still the focus, but the flow becomes **uncontrolled, overwhelming, or tangled in need.** This can lead to jealousy, clinginess, or difficulty maintaining healthy boundaries.

Jealousy: When Love Turns Into Possession

One of the strongest signs of an overactive Heart Chakra is **jealousy.** While the heart's natural state is to expand and include, jealousy contracts. Instead of love flowing freely, it clings, grasps, and guards, fearing that affection or attention might slip away. What begins as love quickly twists into possession.

WHY IT HAPPENS

Jealousy usually arises when the heart is overflowing with desire for love but lacks the grounding of security. Deep down, there is a fear of being **abandoned, replaced, or overlooked.** The heart craves assurance that love is stable, but when that assurance feels missing, insecurity takes its place.

This fear can come from early wounds — being compared to siblings, experiencing betrayal in past relationships, or growing up feeling unseen or unworthy. Instead of trusting love, the heart becomes hyper-alert, scanning for threats and clinging tightly to what it values most.

HOW IT FEELS INSIDE

- **Anxiety** when your partner, friend, or loved one gives attention to someone else.
- **Fear of replacement**, often with the belief that others are "better" or "more deserving" than you.
- **Constant comparison** — measuring yourself against others and feeling you fall short.
- A restless unease, as though love could be taken away at any moment.
- Emotional highs and lows — relief when reassured, panic when reassurance fades.

Inside, jealousy feels like a storm in the chest: pounding heart, shallow breath, and a tightening that makes it hard to rest in trust.

HOW IT APPEARS OUTWARDLY

- **Suspicion:** questioning where someone has been, who they're with, or what they're doing.
- **Control:** trying to limit someone's freedom out of fear that they might leave.
- **Constant reassurance:** needing repeated reminders of love and commitment to feel safe.
- **Overreaction:** small actions by others (a late text, a casual conversation) can trigger outsized emotional responses.

Outwardly, jealousy may look like protectiveness, but underneath, it is driven by insecurity and fear of loss.

THE COST OF JEALOUSY

Jealousy erodes trust — the foundation of all relationships. It creates tension, conflict, and distance, often pushing away the very love it seeks to hold onto. For the person experiencing it, jealousy is exhausting: a constant cycle of fear, reassurance, and doubt. Physically, it can manifest as a racing heartbeat, tight chest, and chronic anxiety.

THE HIDDEN TRUTH

At its core, jealousy is not proof of too much love — it is evidence of **fear inside love.** It is the heart crying out: *"Am I enough? Am I safe? Will love stay?"* Recognizing this truth helps soften jealousy's grip. By shifting from fear to trust, the heart learns that love is not something that can be stolen — it is something that flows, expands, and multiplies when shared.

Clinginess: When Love Becomes Dependency

Another expression of an overactive Heart Chakra is **clinginess.** Instead of love flowing as a gift, it becomes a grasp — a desperate need to hold on so tightly that it overwhelms both giver and receiver. The desire for closeness is natural, but when the heart loses balance, closeness can slip into dependency.

WHY IT HAPPENS

Clinginess usually arises when the heart has not yet learned to feel **whole within itself.** Early experiences of abandonment, inconsistent affection, or conditional love can plant the belief that love is fragile and must be held onto at all costs.

The heart, hungry for reassurance, reaches outward again and again, believing: *"If I don't hold on tightly, love will disappear."* This turns relationships into lifelines, rather than choices born from freedom and joy.

HOW IT FEELS INSIDE

- A constant need for affirmation — "Do you still love me? Do you still care?"
- Fear during times of separation, even brief ones.
- Feeling incomplete or unsafe when alone.
- Anxiety if communication slows or if attention shifts elsewhere.
- Relief only when the connection is re-established, followed by fear that it might vanish again.

Inside, clinginess feels like restlessness, an inability to settle, and a fear that love is never fully secure.

HOW IT APPEARS OUTWARDLY

- **Over-texting or over-calling**, needing frequent contact to feel safe.
- **Over-giving** — offering gifts, favors, or constant attention, hoping it will "earn" love.
- Leaning heavily on others emotionally, making relationships feel one-sided.
- Difficulty respecting personal space, boundaries, or independence.
- Sacrificing your own needs to keep the relationship intact.

While the intention is to hold on to love, the effect can be overwhelming, creating strain and imbalance in the relationship.

THE COST OF CLINGINESS

Clinginess often backfires. The more tightly love is gripped, the more it slips away. Partners or friends may feel smothered, leading to conflict or withdrawal. For the individual, it creates a cycle of anxiety, exhaustion, and dependency, leaving little room for self-love or growth.

Energetically, clinginess drains both the person and their relationships. Instead of the heart radiating freely, its energy collapses inward, constantly seeking reassurance rather than shining outward in trust.

THE HIDDEN TRUTH

Clinginess doesn't come from too much love — it comes from **fear disguised as love.** The heart longs for connection but doesn't yet trust its own completeness. Beneath the grasping is a tender truth: what the heart really wants is safety, stability, and the knowing that love endures.

By learning to find that sense of wholeness within, the heart can shift from dependency to genuine intimacy — from clinging to love, to *becoming love.*

Poor Boundaries: When Compassion Overflows Without Limits

A third sign of an overactive Heart Chakra is **poor boundaries.** While the heart's natural state is to radiate compassion, when it becomes excessive, that compassion spills over without direction. Instead of love flowing in healthy balance, it floods outward — taking on other people's problems, ignoring your own needs, and blurring the line between where you end and others begin.

WHY IT HAPPENS

Poor boundaries often develop when the heart equates love with sacrifice. If you grew up believing that care meant self-denial, or if you learned that your worth depended on pleasing others, the heart may open too widely. This overextension can feel generous at first, but it slowly drains energy, leaving you depleted.

At its core, poor boundaries often come from a **fear of rejection**: *"If I say no, they won't love me."* Instead of honoring both yourself and others, you give endlessly in hopes of maintaining a connection.

HOW IT FEELS INSIDE

- Feeling drained or exhausted after spending time with others.
- Carrying emotions that don't belong to you — sadness, anger, or anxiety picked up from those around you.
- Guilt or fear when you consider saying no.
- A loss of clarity about your own desires, because you are always focused on others.
- A deep but unfulfilled need for reciprocity — wishing someone would care for you the way you care for them.

Inside, poor boundaries feel like being stretched thin, constantly giving but never feeling nourished in return.

HOW IT APPEARS OUTWARDLY

- Always saying yes, even when it hurts or overwhelms you.
- Over-functioning in relationships — doing for others what they could do for themselves.
- Taking on the role of "rescuer" or "fixer," believing it's your responsibility to heal everyone.

- Allowing disrespectful behavior because you fear standing up for yourself might drive people away.
- Rarely asking for help, even when you need it.

Outwardly, poor boundaries can look like endless generosity, but beneath the surface, it's often fueled by fear and self-neglect.

THE COST OF POOR BOUNDARIES

When your heart is wide open without limits, you may end up depleted, resentful, or even ill. Over time, you may experience compassion fatigue, burnout, or physical symptoms in the chest and lungs. Relationships may also suffer, as over-giving creates imbalance and prevents true reciprocity.

THE HIDDEN TRUTH

Poor boundaries are not proof of too much love — they are a sign of **love without direction.** The heart longs to give, but without balance, giving becomes sacrifice. The truth is that saying no does not make love smaller; it makes it clearer, stronger, and more sustainable.

Healthy boundaries are not walls — they are **doors.** They allow love to flow both ways, in and out, without depleting the giver or overwhelming the receiver. When the Heart Chakra is truly balanced, compassion radiates with wisdom, allowing you to love others while still honoring yourself.

The Experience of an Imbalanced Heart

Just as balance in the Heart Chakra is easy to sense, so too is imbalance. Whether you are a practitioner working with clients or a person noticing your own state, the signs of a blocked or overactive heart are clear — though they may show up in different ways.

THE PRACTITIONER'S EXPERIENCE

When scanning or working with someone whose Heart Chakra is imbalanced, a practitioner may notice:

- **Energetic resistance** in the chest — the flow feels jagged, heavy, or collapsed inward.
- The aura around the heart may look or feel **muddy, dull, or streaked with gray, red, or brown**, instead of clear green.
- The energy can feel **hot and restless** (overactive) or **cold and stagnant** (underactive).
- Instead of a smooth rhythm, the energy pulses are irregular, like a drum out of sync.
- The practitioner may feel drained, restless, or even sad while holding space, because the client's field is pulling or pushing energetically rather than flowing in harmony.

Practitioners often sense strong emotions in the client's energy — grief, resentment, fear of abandonment, or the sharpness of jealousy.

THE PERSON'S EXPERIENCE

From the inside, an imbalanced Heart Chakra can be felt in many ways:

- **Emotionally:**
  - Difficulty trusting others.
  - Fear of intimacy or abandonment.
  - Clinging too tightly or shutting down completely.
  - Holding grudges or struggling to forgive.

- o Over-giving to the point of exhaustion, or blocking love altogether.
- **Relationally:**
  - o Relationships may feel strained — either too dependent or too distant.
  - o Patterns of jealousy, possessiveness, or people-pleasing can emerge.
  - o Feeling unseen, unloved, or disconnected, even when surrounded by others.
- **Physically:**
  - o Tightness or heaviness in the chest.
  - o Shallow breathing.
  - o Heart palpitations, blood pressure fluctuations, or recurring colds and lung issues.
- **Spiritually:**
  - o A sense of being cut off from love, God, or the universe.
  - o Difficulty feeling gratitude or seeing beauty in life.
  - o A deep loneliness, even when not physically alone.

RECOGNIZING THE CONTRAST

- A **balanced heart** feels like warmth, openness, and steady compassion.
- An **imbalanced heart** feels like constriction, turbulence, or disconnection.

Both practitioner and person can sense the difference: one radiates peace and love outward, the other struggles to let love flow in or out.

The good news is that an imbalance in the heart is never permanent. With awareness, healing practices, and compassion, Anahata can always return to its natural state of openness and balance.

Chapter 5 – Causes of Disturbance

Childhood Wounds and Relational Trauma

The Heart Chakra is exquisitely sensitive to love, care, and connection. From the moment we are born, the heart learns whether the world is safe, whether love is reliable, and whether we are worthy of affection. For many people, disturbances in Anahata begin not in adulthood, but in the earliest chapters of life.

Early Imprints

During childhood, the heart develops through the relationships we form with parents, caregivers, siblings, and early friends. When those bonds are nurturing, consistent, and safe, the heart learns trust. When they are inconsistent, cold, or painful, the heart learns fear and protection instead.

Even subtle experiences can leave deep marks:

- A parent who withheld affection, leaving the child to wonder if love must be "earned."
- Favoritism or constant comparison to siblings, creating feelings of unworthiness.
- Emotional neglect — being fed and clothed, but rarely hugged or comforted.
- Overprotection, where love was tied to control, leaving little space for individuality.

These experiences may not always look dramatic, but they teach the heart patterns of doubt, shame, or fear that echo into adulthood.

Relational Trauma

Relational trauma goes beyond childhood. It can occur in adolescence or adulthood through painful experiences such as:

- **Betrayal:** being cheated on, lied to, or abandoned by someone deeply trusted.
- **Abuse:** emotional manipulation, verbal attacks, or physical harm that breaks the sense of safety.
- **Loss:** the death of a loved one, divorce, or sudden separation that leaves the heart raw and unprotected.
- **Toxic dynamics:** relationships that cycle through love and rejection, creating instability and confusion.

These traumas often plant hidden beliefs like:

- *"Love isn't safe."*
- *"I'll always be left."*
- *"I'm not good enough to be loved."*

The heart, in its attempt to survive, responds by closing down (blocked/deficient) or grasping too tightly (overactive).

How These Wounds Shape the Heart

- **Blocked/Deficient Heart:** Fear of intimacy, isolation, and bitterness often grow from early neglect or betrayal. The heart learns to wall itself off for protection.
- **Overactive Heart:** Clinginess, jealousy, and poor boundaries often stem from inconsistent love or abandonment. The heart grasps too tightly to avoid losing love again.

- **Physical Echoes:** These wounds may also show up in the body — tightness in the chest, shallow breathing, heart palpitations, or weakened immunity.

The Hidden Truth

Childhood wounds and relational trauma do not mean the heart is permanently broken. The Heart Chakra is resilient — it can soften, reopen, and restore balance when given care, safety, and compassion. Healing begins with recognizing these early patterns, not to blame the past, but to free the present.

Grief, Loss, and Unresolved Heartbreak

If childhood wounds plant the seeds of disturbance in the Heart Chakra, then grief and heartbreak are the storms that can shake it to its core. Few experiences impact Anahata as profoundly as the loss of love — whether through death, separation, or the end of a cherished relationship.

The Weight of Grief

Grief is the natural response to losing someone or something we love. It is the heart's way of acknowledging that what once filled it is no longer physically present. While grief itself is not "bad" — it is an expression of love — when it remains unresolved, it can cause the heart's energy to collapse inward.

- **How it feels inside:** heaviness in the chest, a dull ache, or the sensation of a "broken heart."
- **How it appears outwardly:** loss of interest in life, emotional withdrawal, difficulty trusting joy again.
- **Energetically:** the heart chakra may feel dim, constricted, or weighed down, as if light cannot pass through.

Loss and Its Echoes

Loss comes in many forms:

- **Death:** the passing of a loved one leaves an emptiness that feels impossible to fill.
- **Breakups or divorce:** losing a romantic partner can make the heart fear love itself.
- **Friendship loss or betrayal:** when trust is broken, the heart learns caution instead of openness.
- **Life transitions:** moving away, children growing up, or the loss of a home or career can all touch the heart.

Each loss tells the heart: *"Love is gone."* Without healing, that message can become a hidden belief that love itself is unsafe or fleeting.

Unresolved Heartbreak

Heartbreak differs from grief in that it often carries layers of longing, regret, or self-blame. Where grief eventually moves toward acceptance, heartbreak can leave the heart **stuck in the past** — replaying what was lost, what went wrong, or what might have been.

Signs of unresolved heartbreak include:

- Difficulty moving on, even years after the event.
- Fear of opening the heart again.
- Constant comparison of new relationships to the one that ended.
- Emotional numbness, as if the heart has shut down to avoid further pain.

How Grief and Heartbreak Disturb Anahata

- **Blocked/Deficient:** The heart closes down, leading to isolation, coldness, or fear of intimacy.
- **Overactive:** The heart clings desperately, leading to jealousy, clinginess, or over-giving to avoid abandonment.
- **Physical Echoes:** Many people feel grief physically — tightness in the chest, shallow breathing, immune suppression, or even chest pain.

The Hidden Truth

Grief and heartbreak are not signs that love is gone — they are proof that love existed. The very pain of loss shows the depth of connection the heart once felt. The danger comes only when grief is suppressed or heartbreak left unresolved.

The Heart Chakra is designed to heal. With time, compassion, and practices that gently reopen Anahata, the same energy that once felt broken can become a source of deeper wisdom, empathy, and strength.

Ancestral Patterns Carried in the Heart Field

The Heart Chakra does not exist in isolation. It is part of a living web of energy that stretches across generations. Just as we inherit eye color or facial features, we also inherit **emotional imprints and relational patterns** through what is often called the *heart field.*

These ancestral patterns are not destiny, but they do create energetic tendencies that shape how we experience love, trust, and connection.

How Ancestral Energy Reaches Us

- **Family stories and beliefs:** If generations before you believed love had to be earned, endured betrayal, or carried bitterness, those beliefs can subtly pass down.
- **Emotional inheritance:** Children often absorb the unspoken emotions of their parents — grief, fear, or unprocessed trauma — and carry them forward.
- **Epigenetics:** Modern science shows that trauma can influence gene expression, meaning emotional wounds may echo in the body across multiple generations.
- **Energetic lineage:** Many energy healers describe the heart field as containing threads of memory, like echoes that stretch back through time.

Signs of Ancestral Heart Patterns

You may be carrying ancestral patterns if you notice:

- Repeated relationship struggles across generations (divorce, betrayal, loss).
- Family tendencies toward closed-off emotions, lack of affection, or difficulty expressing love.
- An inherited sense of shame, guilt, or unworthiness without a clear personal cause.
- Feeling grief or heaviness in the chest that doesn't seem to "belong" to your own life experiences.

How It Disturbs the Heart Chakra

- **Blocked/Deficient:** Generational trauma may cause the heart to stay closed — repeating cycles of isolation, bitterness, or fear of intimacy.
- **Overactive:** Family wounds may create patterns of clinging, over-giving, or blurred boundaries as a way to prevent abandonment.

- **Physical:** Families may even share physical heart or lung conditions, reflecting unprocessed emotional burdens.

The Hidden Truth

Ancestral patterns are not chains, but **echoes.** They are carried forward only until someone chooses to heal them. When you recognize and release ancestral burdens in your heart, you not only free yourself — you also free your lineage, past and future.

The Heart Chakra is uniquely suited to this work because it holds the power of forgiveness, compassion, and unconditional love. Through Anahata, you can heal not only your own wounds but also those carried silently for generations.

Environmental and Energetic Toxins: Stress, Fear, and Societal Conditioning

Even if your childhood was loving and your relationships are healthy, the Heart Chakra is still influenced by the **environment you live in** and the **energies you're surrounded by.** Just as the physical heart responds to diet, air quality, and exercise, the energetic heart responds to the quality of your thoughts, surroundings, and collective culture.

Stress and Overstimulation

Modern life bombards the heart with constant stimulation. Fast-paced schedules, long work hours, financial worries, and digital overload keep the nervous system in a near-constant state of fight-or-flight.

- **Effect on the heart:** Chronic stress tightens the chest, quickens the heartbeat, and restricts breathing.

Energetically, this creates a jittery, overcharged field around Anahata, making it harder to stay calm and open.
- **Signs you might notice:** irritability, shallow breathing, feeling "wired but tired," difficulty feeling compassion or patience.

Fear and Collective Anxiety

We are also exposed to fear on a collective level — news cycles, social media, political tension, or global crises. Even if these events aren't happening directly to you, the emotional charge in the collective field can seep into your heart.

- **Effect on the heart:** Fear causes contraction. The aura around the heart may feel dimmer, denser, or prickly. Compassion turns inward for protection, making it harder to stay open.
- **Signs you might notice:** a sense of heaviness in the chest after scrolling news, sudden loss of trust in others, or feeling unsafe without a clear reason.

Societal Conditioning

From a young age, most of us are taught subtle messages about how to handle our hearts:

- "Don't cry."
- "Be strong."
- "Don't be too sensitive."
- "Love has to be earned."

These beliefs act like **energetic toxins** in the heart field. They teach us to suppress emotions, hide vulnerability, and treat openness as weakness. Over time, this conditioning can block the Heart Chakra just as surely as personal trauma.

- **Effect on the heart:** The natural flow of feeling and expression gets interrupted. Compassion may be replaced by cynicism, authenticity by performance.
- **Signs you might notice:** difficulty crying, feeling numb or disconnected, mistrusting your own emotions, or believing that softness equals weakness.

How Environmental and Energetic Toxins Disturb Anahata

- **Blocked/Deficient:** Constant stress or societal conditioning can make the heart close down to cope — leading to isolation, apathy, or emotional numbness.
- **Overactive:** Fear and overstimulation can make the heart overextend — leading to burnout, over-giving, or constant emotional reactivity.
- **Physical:** Chronic stress hormones strain the cardiovascular and respiratory systems, mirroring the energetic imbalance.

The Hidden Truth

Your heart field is porous. It interacts constantly with the energy around you. But this doesn't mean you're powerless — it means you can choose what you expose your heart to and how you care for it. Just as you wouldn't drink polluted water, you can limit the "energetic toxins" you take in by practicing boundaries, mindfulness, and heart-centered grounding.

By recognizing the effect of stress, fear, and conditioning, you take the first step to clearing and protecting the Heart Chakra — giving it the space it needs to radiate compassion and vitality again.

Chapter 6 – Signs of Balance

Emotional Harmony: Empathy, Acceptance, and Peace

When the Heart Chakra is balanced, you feel it first in your emotions. Unlike sudden bursts of happiness that come and go, Anahata's balance creates a steady emotional foundation — a calm rhythm of openness, kindness, and compassion that underlies your daily life.

Empathy: Feeling With, Not Just For

When the Heart Chakra is balanced, empathy flows naturally. Empathy is more than sympathy or pity — it is the ability to **feel with someone, not just for them**. It allows you to recognize another's joy or sorrow as real and valid, while still remembering that their experience does not erase your own center.

A balanced heart acts like a tuning fork. It resonates with the emotions of others, vibrating in harmony with their feelings, but it doesn't crack or break under the strain. You sense what they feel without becoming lost in it. Their pain awakens your compassion, not your despair; their joy uplifts you without sparking jealousy.

IN PRACTICE

- You find yourself truly listening, not rushing to give advice or fix the problem, but simply being present.
- You can sit with someone's grief, allowing silence and presence to speak louder than words.
- In conversation, even when you disagree, you remain anchored in respect for their worth as a person.
- Your own emotions stay steady, so you don't feel drained after offering support.

THE DIFFERENCE

Empathy is not the same as absorbing or carrying another person's emotions. That would be an imbalance — over-identifying with their pain until you feel exhausted or overwhelmed. True empathy allows you to stay in your own energy while offering a safe, steady space for others.

This is why a balanced Heart Chakra makes you a **safe witness**. You don't try to control, fix, or take away someone's experience. Instead, you offer presence, compassion, and acceptance — the greatest gifts a heart can give.

THE RIPPLE EFFECT

Empathy doesn't just help the person you're connecting with — it also changes you. By feeling with another, you expand your own capacity for love and understanding. Empathy softens judgment, dissolves separation, and reminds you that beneath our differences, we share the same humanity.

In this way, a balanced Heart Chakra creates healing on both sides: the person who is seen and heard feels less alone, and the one offering empathy feels more connected to life itself.

Acceptance: Allowing Life to Be What It Is

A balanced Heart Chakra brings the gift of acceptance. Acceptance is often misunderstood — it doesn't mean pretending that everything is perfect, or that harmful behavior is okay. Instead, it means **letting go of the struggle to control life** and learning to meet yourself and others with honesty and compassion.

When the heart is open, you can see flaws, mistakes, and wounds without turning away. You can accept your own humanity without shame and accept the humanity of others without demanding they be different. This doesn't weaken your boundaries or your values; rather, it frees you from the exhausting habit of resistance.

IN PRACTICE

- You stop fighting with reality, even when it is uncomfortable. Instead of resisting what is, you face it with courage and openness.
- You acknowledge your emotions honestly — anger, sadness, joy, fear — without condemning yourself for feeling them.
- You allow others to walk their own paths, even when their choices are different from what you would choose. You no longer carry the heavy need to change them in order to feel safe or whole.
- You release the grip of perfectionism, recognizing that growth happens through trial, error, and compassion.

THE GIFT OF ACCEPTANCE

Acceptance creates space for healing — both in yourself and in your relationships. When people feel accepted, they naturally relax, soften, and open. What seemed rigid begins to bend. What felt closed begins to unfold.

For you, acceptance brings peace. You no longer waste energy on constant resistance or judgment. You become more present, more grounded, and more able to respond with wisdom instead of reactivity.

ACCEPTANCE AND THE HEART CHAKRA

In energy terms, resistance tightens the chest, contracts breath, and constricts the aura around the heart. Acceptance, on the other hand, feels like **space opening inside and around you.** The heart expands, breath flows more freely, and your energy field feels warmer and more inviting.

Through acceptance, the Heart Chakra returns to its natural rhythm — a steady pulse of compassion that embraces life as it is, while gently guiding it toward growth.

Peace: The Calm at the Center

One of the clearest signs of a balanced Heart Chakra is an abiding sense of peace. This peace is not the absence of problems or challenges — it is the quiet knowing that you are **held by love, even in the midst of uncertainty.** It is the still point at the center of the wheel, the calm eye within the storm.

When Anahata is open, you no longer swing wildly between highs and lows. Instead, your emotions flow in a steady rhythm, anchored by the heart's stability. Peace becomes less about what is happening around you and more about what is alive within you.

- You feel resilient in the face of life's challenges. Difficulties still come, but they don't throw you as far off course.
- Conflicts don't pull you into drama as easily. You may still feel anger or sadness, but you return to balance more quickly.
- Gratitude rises naturally, even in small moments — a smile from a stranger, sunlight on your skin, the sound of laughter.
- You can rest in the present moment without constantly worrying about the future or replaying the past.

THE GIFT OF PEACE

Peace in the heart is not only for you — it radiates outward. Others feel calmer in your presence, even without words. Your aura becomes steady, like a **gentle rhythm guiding the room.** In relationships, your peace becomes a safe harbor for others, reminding them that they too can soften, breathe, and find their center.

This kind of peace is deeply magnetic. People may not be able to explain it, but they are drawn to the steadiness of a balanced heart. Your very presence becomes healing.

PEACE AND THE HEART CHAKRA

Energetically, peace shows up as a **smooth, even flow through the chest and aura.** The green of Anahata shines clear and radiant, sometimes touched with pink or gold, reflecting unconditional love. The breath deepens naturally, and the body relaxes into a state of ease.

This peace is not fragile — it is strong. It is the kind of peace that allows you to meet life as it is, with courage, openness, and love.

Living in Emotional Harmony

When empathy, acceptance, and peace flow together, the heart becomes more than an energy center — it becomes a **sanctuary.** In this space, you are no longer swept away by every surge of emotion, whether your own or those of others. Instead, you stand rooted in compassion, steady and open, able to meet life with grace.

This harmony doesn't mean you stop feeling. You will still experience joy and sorrow, delight and disappointment — but you will no longer be ruled by them. Your emotions become like waves on the surface of a deep, calm sea. The waves rise and fall, yet the ocean of your heart remains vast, steady, and whole.

IN PRACTICE

- In relationships, you can love without clinging and forgive without losing yourself.
- In daily life, challenges feel less like threats and more like opportunities to grow.
- In your inner world, your thoughts soften, your body relaxes, and gratitude becomes a natural rhythm.

THE GIFT OF HARMONY

When the heart lives in harmony, it uplifts not only you, but everyone you encounter. Others sense your steadiness. They feel safer, calmer, and more open simply by being in your presence. This is not because you are perfect or free from struggle, but because you are anchored in love.

Balancing the Heart Chakra in this way doesn't erase pain or conflict. Life will still bring its storms. But harmony gives you the strength to walk through those storms with dignity. You are no longer reacting from fear or closing yourself off in defense — you are meeting life with the courage of love.

This is the true power of Anahata: not to escape life, but to **live fully within it**, guided by compassion, acceptance, and peace.

Physical Health of the Heart and Lungs

The Heart Chakra is not only a center of love and compassion — it is also deeply connected to the **physical organs of the chest: the heart and the lungs.** These two organs work together to sustain life, and their health often mirrors the state of your emotional and energetic heart.

THE PHYSICAL HEART

Your physical heart is the tireless muscle that pumps blood through your entire body, delivering oxygen and nutrients to every cell. It is both a physical organ and a powerful symbol of life itself.

When the Heart Chakra is balanced, many people notice their **heart feels strong and steady**. They may experience healthy blood pressure, stable circulation, and an overall sense of vitality.

When Anahata is imbalanced, however, issues of the heart often arise:

- Palpitations or irregular heartbeat
- High or low blood pressure
- Blockages in circulation
- Chest tightness or pain

- A higher risk of cardiovascular disease

Energetically, emotional stress, grief, and resentment can weigh heavily on the heart. Over time, these emotional burdens may manifest physically, showing how deeply connected the chakra system is to overall health.

THE LUNGS

The lungs are the partner to the heart, drawing in oxygen and releasing carbon dioxide. In energy terms, the lungs are associated with **breath, life force (prana, qi, or ki), and the ability to take life in and let go.**

A balanced Heart Chakra supports lungs that feel open and expansive, making breathing easier and fuller. Imbalances, however, may show up as:

- Shortness of breath or shallow breathing
- Asthma or allergies
- Respiratory infections or chronic cough
- A sense of heaviness in the chest when grieving or holding back emotions

In Traditional Chinese Medicine, the lungs are linked with the emotion of **grief.** When grief is unprocessed, the chest can feel tight and constricted, directly mirroring an imbalanced heart chakra.

THE HEART–LUNG CONNECTION

The heart and lungs work in a sacred partnership: the lungs bring in oxygen, and the heart pumps it through the bloodstream. One cannot thrive without the other. Similarly, the Heart Chakra is about **connection and balance** — between giving and receiving, holding and releasing, loving and letting go.

This connection shows up in breath practices. Deep, slow breathing naturally calms the heart rate and supports cardiovascular health, while shallow, rapid breathing can strain the heart and keep the body in a state of stress.

SUPPORTING HEART AND LUNG HEALTH

Balancing the Heart Chakra can directly support these organs through both physical and energetic practices:

- **Breathwork:** Deep breathing, pranayama, or mindful breath practices expand lung capacity and calm the heart.
- **Movement:** Gentle cardiovascular exercise (walking, yoga, tai chi, qigong) keeps both heart and lungs strong.
- **Emotional Release:** Allowing grief, sadness, or resentment to move through you prevents the chest from "locking down."
- **Reiki/Energy Work:** Placing hands over the sternum or back of the chest encourages flow through both organs.
- **Affirmations:** Phrases such as *"My heart and lungs are strong and filled with life"* reinforce balance on the mental-emotional level.

The Body as a Mirror of the Heart

When your Heart Chakra is open, the heart and lungs function with greater ease. Breathing feels freer, circulation feels stronger, and your whole body benefits from better oxygen and energy flow. When Anahata is blocked, the body often mirrors it with tightness, imbalance, or fatigue in the chest.

Your physical heart and lungs are living reflections of your energetic heart. By caring for one, you naturally support the other.

Spiritual Qualities: Unconditional Love, Unity, and Divine Connection

At its deepest level, the Heart Chakra is not just about emotions or relationships — it is the **gateway to spiritual love.** When Anahata is open and balanced, it awakens qualities that transcend personal feelings and connect you to something greater than yourself.

UNCONDITIONAL LOVE

The highest expression of Anahata is unconditional love — love that does not depend on circumstances, perfection, or reciprocity. It is the love that remains steady, whether or not someone agrees with you, whether life is easy or difficult.

- **In practice:** You may feel warmth in your chest that expands outward without effort, touching everyone and everything around you. This love isn't limited to family or friends — it includes strangers, animals, nature, and even yourself.
- **The gift:** When you embody unconditional love, you become less reactive and more forgiving. You realize that love is not something you "get" or "lose" — it is something you *are*.

UNITY

The heart is the place where separation dissolves. In its balanced state, the Heart Chakra reveals that beneath our differences — race, culture, beliefs, or roles — we are all part of one human family, woven together by life itself.

- **In practice:** You may feel a natural sense of kinship with others, even those very different from you. Acts of kindness feel like a natural extension of yourself rather than an effort.

- **The gift:** Unity brings peace. It dissolves the illusion of isolation and shows you that the same energy flowing through your heart also flows through the hearts of others.

DIVINE CONNECTION

The Heart Chakra is often described as the meeting place of the human and the divine. When it is fully awakened, you may sense the presence of something greater — whether you call it God, Spirit, Source, or simply Love itself.

- **In practice:** During meditation or prayer, you may feel surrounded by light, held in grace, or touched by a profound stillness that goes beyond words.
- **The gift:** This connection brings trust. You begin to feel guided and supported by life itself, even during challenges. The more you rest in this connection, the more your life becomes an expression of divine love in action.

The Experience of a Balanced Heart

Balance in the Heart Chakra can be felt both from the **inside** (your own lived experience) and from the **outside** (how a healer or practitioner perceives it). Together, these perspectives create a fuller picture of what heart-centered harmony looks like in real life.

THE PRACTITIONER'S EXPERIENCE

When a Reiki or energy practitioner works with someone whose Heart Chakra is balanced, the difference is palpable:

- The energy in the chest feels **smooth, steady, and warm**, with no sudden breaks or resistance.
- The aura around the heart radiates **clear green light**, sometimes tinged with rose or gold. It feels expansive, not collapsed or spiky.
- The rhythm of energy flow is **consistent**, like a gentle, even pulse that synchronizes easily with the practitioner's own hands.
- Sessions often feel uplifting for the practitioner as well — they leave not drained, but inspired and calm, as if they too have bathed in the client's open-hearted energy.

Balanced heart energy is magnetic. Practitioners often describe feeling drawn into a field of compassion that makes the session more than a technique — it becomes a shared space of healing presence.

THE PERSON'S EXPERIENCE

For the individual, a balanced Heart Chakra feels like being at home within themselves:

- **Emotionally:** They feel lighter, freer, and more accepting of their own imperfections. Forgiveness (of self and others) comes more easily.
- **Relationally:** They feel connected yet not dependent — able to give love without losing themselves and to receive love without fear.
- **Physically:** The chest feels open, breathing is fuller, and tension in the shoulders and ribs often melts away.

- **Spiritually:** They sense a quiet presence, a feeling of being supported by something greater than themselves. Gratitude and peace rise naturally.

Instead of chasing love or fearing rejection, they live from a place of **inner sufficiency**. Love becomes not something to earn, but something to express.

THE DEEPER LESSONS OF ANAHATA

Beyond its colors, symbols, and practices, the Heart Chakra whispers lessons that are often felt more than spoken. These lessons aren't about techniques — they are about the truths that slowly reshape how we live.

- **Love:** Not just romance, not just kindness, but the kind of love that says *yes* to life, even when it is difficult. Love that does not demand perfection, but embraces humanity in all its rawness.
- **Compassion:** The ability to feel another's experience without losing yourself. Compassion is strength, not weakness. It is the quiet power that allows us to stand in the presence of suffering without turning away.
- **Balance:** The heart teaches that giving and receiving are two halves of one breath. Too much of either creates distortion, but in balance, love flows freely.

These are not always easy lessons. They ask us to soften when we want to harden, to forgive when we want to cling, to remain open when life tempts us to close. Yet every time we choose love, compassion, and balance, even in small ways, we re-align with the deepest truth of Anahata: **that love is not something we earn, but something we are.**

WHY THIS MATTERS

When both practitioner and client experience the heart in balance, healing unfolds in a way that is effortless. The practitioner feels safe and guided by love; the client feels seen, held, and more connected to their true self. This is the gift of Anahata: it harmonizes the healer and the healed, reminding both that love is the essence of all transformation.

Living from the Spiritual Heart

When unconditional love, unity, and divine connection come alive in Anahata, the heart becomes a **temple within you.** It is no longer just about personal healing, but about radiating a love that uplifts the world around you.

This is the ultimate lesson of the Heart Chakra: love is not only an emotion — it is a **state of being**. To live from the spiritual heart is to embody compassion, forgiveness, and trust as a way of life, shining as a reminder that love is the true essence of the soul.

Chapter 7 – Hidden Secrets & Esoteric Wisdom

Tantra and the Heart Chakra

When we speak of Anahata in its original context, we are speaking the language of **Tantra.**

What is Tantra?

- The word *Tantra* comes from Sanskrit roots: **"tan"** (to expand) and **"tra"** (to liberate or weave). Together, it means *a system of expansion and liberation* — a way of weaving body, mind, and spirit into wholeness.
- Tantra arose in India thousands of years ago as a set of practices that honored both the physical and the spiritual. Unlike ascetic traditions that rejected the body, Tantra saw the human being as a microcosm of the universe. The body was not an obstacle to enlightenment — it was the temple where enlightenment could be realized.

The Tantric Map of the Chakras

- It was within Tantra that the **chakra system** first appeared in detail — described in early scriptures such as the *Yoga Upanishads* and developed fully in Tantric texts like the *Shat Chakra Nirupana* (circa 16th century, based on earlier oral teachings).

- In these teachings, the chakras were seen as **energy centers (lotuses)** along the central channel (*sushumna nadi*), each with its own petals, deities, colors, seed sounds (bija mantras), and elements.
- The chakras were not abstract ideas, but **maps for meditation and inner awakening.** By visualizing their symbols, chanting their mantras, and awakening their energies, practitioners sought to unlock higher states of consciousness.

Tantra and Anahata

- In the Tantric vision, Anahata — the Heart Chakra — was the **gateway lotus**. It united the lower centers of survival, creativity, and power with the upper centers of expression, intuition, and spiritual union.
- Tantric texts describe Anahata as the seat of the *unstruck sound* (Anahata Nada) — the vibration that exists eternally within, without being created by two things striking together. Meditating here was said to open the inner ear to the music of the cosmos.

It is also here that Tantra places its deities: **Ishvara** (the cosmic Self, pure consciousness) and **Kakini** (the Shakti of the heart, nurturing and devotional). These were not "gods" in the Western sense, but **living archetypes within the practitioner, awakened through meditation and mantra.**

Why This Matters Today

Modern Reiki, yoga, and energy healing have borrowed chakra teachings, often simplifying them into colors and traits. But in Tantra, the chakras were **alive** — multidimensional temples within the subtle body, each with guardians, sounds, animals, and cosmic truths. To approach the Heart Chakra in this way is to step into its original sacred context: not just as an "energy point," but as a doorway into the divine mystery within your own being.

CHAKRAS AND KUNDALINI IN TANTRA
What is Kundalini?

- In Tantric philosophy, **Kundalini** is the **dormant spiritual energy** coiled at the base of the spine, often symbolized as a sleeping serpent.
- When awakened (through practices like meditation, breathwork, mantra, or initiation), Kundalini rises upward through the central channel (*sushumna nadi*), passing through each chakra in turn.
- As she ascends, each chakra "lotus" is activated, unfolding its petals, awakening its qualities, and clearing its blockages.

The Role of the Heart Chakra in Kundalini's Ascent

- When Kundalini reaches **Anahata, the Heart Chakra**, it marks a **turning point** in the journey.
- In the lower chakras, Kundalini energy activates physical, emotional, and personal powers (survival, sexuality, will). But in the heart, she awakens **love, compassion, and devotion** — the qualities that bridge the human and the divine.
- Many texts describe the heart as the place where Kundalini meets **Ishvara (the inner Self)** — a moment of deep inner recognition, where the seeker begins to experience themselves as more than body and mind.
- This is why many practitioners report experiences of overwhelming love, bliss, or unity when Kundalini touches the heart.

Tantric Symbolism of Anahata in Kundalini Practice

- **The "Unstruck Sound" (Anahata Nada):** Yogis say that when Kundalini awakens the heart, one begins to hear the inner sound current — a mystical vibration like a flute, bell, or hum, said to come from beyond the physical world.
- **The Flame in the Heart Cave:** The *Hridaya Guha* (heart cave) becomes illuminated, and the eternal flame of the Self can be directly experienced.
- **Union of Shakti and Shiva:** In the heart, the rising Shakti energy begins to taste the presence of Shiva (pure consciousness) — their union is glimpsed, foreshadowing the full merger at the crown chakra.

Kundalini Awakening and the Heart in Practice

- For some, Kundalini rising to the heart can bring **ecstatic love and deep healing.**
- For others, it may surface **grief, old wounds, or fears of intimacy** that must be released before the heart can fully open.
- This is why Tantra emphasizes that the heart is not just a "stop along the way" — it is a **gateway of transformation.** Without opening the heart, Kundalini's ascent remains incomplete.

Energy Gateways: The Physical Heart vs. the Spiritual Heart

In most chakra teachings, we speak of the Heart Chakra — **Anahata** — located at the center of the chest, radiating green energy, and connected to love, balance, and compassion. But in some spiritual traditions, there is said to be a **second, deeper layer** known as the *"spiritual heart."*

The Physical Heart Chakra (Anahata)

- Located at the sternum, between the lungs.
- Governs the flow of love in human relationships: compassion, forgiveness, empathy, and self-love.
- Connects the lower chakras (physical survival, creativity, will) with the upper chakras (expression, intuition, spirit).

Often described as the "bridge" in the seven-chakra **system.**

The Spiritual Heart (Hridaya or Inner Heart)

- Spoken of in **Tantric and Vedantic texts,** as well as in Sufi mysticism and Christian contemplative prayer.
- Said to reside slightly deeper and to the right of the physical heart chakra — not a chakra in itself, but a gateway to the soul.
- Associated with unconditional, universal love — love beyond personal attachment.
- Often described as the place where divine presence (God, Spirit, Source) meets human consciousness.

Different Traditions, Same Truth

- **Yoga & Tantra:** The *Hridaya* is the "cave of the heart," where the eternal Self (Atman) dwells.

- **Sufism:** The *qalb* (heart) is the seat of divine remembrance.
- **Christian Mysticism:** The "Sacred Heart" is the indwelling presence of Christ within.
- **Modern Energy Work:** Practitioners may sense this as a deeper layer within Anahata, felt as radiant stillness or a pulsing light.

Working with the Two Gateways

- **Physical Heart Chakra Practice:** Focus on relationships, forgiveness, healing grief, and balancing giving/receiving love.
- **Spiritual Heart Practice:** Meditate by turning awareness inward, as if moving behind or inside the heart center. Rest in silence there. Many describe this as entering a boundless space of peace and unity.

The Gift of the Spiritual Heart

Understanding this distinction helps practitioners go deeper. The **Heart Chakra** teaches us how to love as humans. The **Spiritual Heart** reminds us that love is eternal, beyond personality or story. Together, they show us that healing the heart is both **personal and universal.**

Karmic Lessons: Repeating Heart Wounds Across Lifetimes

WHAT IS KARMA?
Literal Meaning

- *Karma* comes from the Sanskrit root **"kri"** meaning *to act, to do, to create.*

- At its simplest, karma means **action.** But in spiritual philosophy, it refers not only to the action itself but also to its **consequence or ripple.**

The Law of Cause and Effect

- Just as a stone dropped into water creates ripples, every thought, word, and deed creates an **energetic ripple** that eventually returns to the doer.
- This doesn't mean "punishment" or "reward" from outside — karma is more like **the natural law of balance,** similar to gravity. What is set in motion will, in time, find its way back.

Types of Karma (from Yogic & Tantric Teachings)

1. **Sanchita Karma** – the accumulated karma from all lifetimes, the big storehouse of seeds.
2. **Prarabdha Karma** – the portion of karma chosen for this lifetime, shaping circumstances like birth, family, and major life lessons.
3. **Kriyamana Karma** – the karma we are creating right now through choices and actions.
4. **Agami Karma** – future karma, the seeds being planted for lifetimes ahead.

Karma and the Heart Chakra

- Many teachings say the **heart is where karmic imprints are carried.** Old grief, unresolved wounds, ancestral pain — all of these can sit like weights in Anahata.
- When the heart is healed and opened, those karmic patterns can be released, dissolved, or transformed into wisdom.
- This is why forgiveness practices, compassion meditations, and love-based energy work are considered

karmic medicine. They don't just ease the present moment; they **untie knots carried across lifetimes.**

Beyond "Good" and "Bad"

In the West, karma often gets simplified to "do good, get good; do bad, get bad." But in deeper yogic and Tantric philosophy:

- Karma isn't about morality — it's about **energy in motion.**
- Its purpose is not to punish but to **teach and liberate.** Every karmic ripple eventually guides us back to wholeness.

The Goal: Freedom from Karma

Through awareness, meditation, and heart-centered living, one can begin to act from **love and clarity instead of fear or attachment.** Such action is said to create little to no karma because it flows in harmony with truth.

- This state is called **Karma Yoga** — living as love in action.
- When the heart leads, karma becomes less about cycles of pain and more about **cycles of awakening.**

The Heart Chakra is not only shaped by the experiences of this lifetime — it also carries echoes of the past. Many traditions teach that unresolved grief, betrayal, or fear of love can ripple forward across generations or even lifetimes. These patterns become karmic lessons, returning again and again until they are brought into the light of awareness and compassion.

REPEATING HEART WOUNDS ACROSS LIFETIMES

- **What it means:** Karmic lessons are unresolved patterns of love and relationships that reappear in different

forms. A soul may face repeated experiences of abandonment, betrayal, or unfulfilled love until the deeper lesson is learned.
- **How it shows up:**
  - Feeling an *instant recognition* (positive or painful) when meeting certain people.
  - Repeating cycles of heartbreak, jealousy, or isolation despite different partners or settings.
  - A deep longing for a "lost love" that feels bigger than this life.
- **Healing path:** Past life regression, karmic Reiki, or meditation on the Heart Chakra can reveal and release these imprints, allowing love to flow freely in the present.

Clearing Ancestral Grief

- **What it means:** Just as DNA carries physical traits, energy fields can carry emotional imprints from ancestors. If generations before you experienced war, loss, or heartbreak, those unhealed sorrows may live on in your heart field.
- **How it shows up:**
  - Inherited family patterns of broken relationships or mistrust.
  - Chronic grief, heaviness, or fear of intimacy without a clear cause.
  - Feeling burdened by sadness that doesn't seem entirely your own.
- **Healing path:**
  - Use Reiki or meditation to intentionally connect with your lineage and send healing love back through the family line.
  - Light a candle for ancestors, offering forgiveness and release.
  - Affirm: *"This grief ends with me. I carry forward only love."*

Why the Heart Holds Karma

The heart is the soul's bridge between human and divine experience. When love is blocked or distorted, its lessons must repeat until the soul remembers its true nature: love without condition, fear, or attachment. Each act of forgiveness, compassion, or boundary-setting not only heals you, but also **heals backwards and forwards** — across past lives, ancestors, and future generations.

The Gift of Karmic Healing

When you clear karmic heart wounds, you free yourself from old cycles of pain and create space for new, healthier expressions of love. In doing so, you also become a healer for your lineage and, ultimately, a clearer channel of compassion for the collective.

Secret Uses of the Heart Chakra: Astral Travel, Sound Meditation, and Awakening Higher Consciousness

The Heart Chakra is often taught as the center of love and compassion — and it is. But in the deeper streams of yogic and mystical practice, Anahata was also seen as a **gateway to subtle realms of awareness.** This is where its "hidden" or "esoteric" uses come into play.

ASTRAL TRAVEL: THE HEART AS A GATEWAY

Many traditions — from Indian yoga to Tibetan Buddhism to Western mysticism — describe the heart as the *seat of the subtle body.* In these teachings, the heart is not only an energy center but a **portal between dimensions of consciousness.**

Practitioners believed that, when the Heart Chakra is deeply balanced and awakened, the subtle body can separate from the physical body more easily for astral travel or lucid dreaming. Instead of feeling "out of control," the journey remains tethered to the heart — like a lighthouse guiding the traveler back home.

- **Why the heart?** In mystical texts, the heart is described as the place where the soul resides while incarnate. Traveling from the heart, rather than the mind, was believed to keep experiences loving, stable, and protected.

SOUND MEDITATION: HEARING THE "UNSTRUCK SOUND"

The Sanskrit name *Anahata* means "unstruck sound" — a vibration that arises without two things colliding. Mystics interpreted this as an **inner sound or hum** that can be heard in deep meditation.

- Some practitioners describe it as a soft flute, a gentle bell, or a deep cosmic hum.
- Others experience it as a rhythm like a heartbeat, steady and endless.

By tuning into this "unstruck sound," meditators believed they could align their own vibration with the universal heartbeat — a practice said to dissolve restlessness, awaken compassion, and open subtle channels of intuition.

AWAKENING HIGHER CONSCIOUSNESS

In esoteric yoga, the Heart Chakra is not the end of the journey — it is the **bridge.** Once balanced, it allows the energy of the lower chakras to rise upward to the higher centers (throat, third eye, crown), supporting spiritual insight and states of unity consciousness.

- Through practices like pranayama (breath control), bija mantras (seed sounds), and heart-centered meditation, practitioners would awaken Anahata to act as a "launch pad" for expanded awareness.
- When the heart is open, higher consciousness doesn't feel abstract or detached — it feels **embodied in compassion, grounded in love.**

This was considered the "safe" way to open higher centers: through the heart first, ensuring that any expanded awareness is guided by empathy and balance rather than ego.

THE HIDDEN TEACHING

In all these secret uses — astral travel, sound meditation, awakening higher states — the heart is both **anchor and portal.** It grounds you in love while opening you to infinite awareness. Without the heart, mystical practices can become unbalanced or overwhelming. With the heart, they become transformative, integrating spirit and humanity into one harmonious field.

Western Mysticism: Christ Consciousness and Kabbalah's Tiferet

Though the chakra system comes from India, the wisdom of the heart is not confined to the East. In Western mysticism, too, the heart has been honored as the center of love, harmony, and divine connection. Two powerful parallels stand out: **Christ consciousness** and **Kabbalah's Tiferet.**

CHRIST CONSCIOUSNESS: THE HEART AS THE DWELLING PLACE OF LOVE

In Christian mysticism, the heart is often described as the true dwelling place of Christ. Saints, monks, and contemplatives have written about experiencing the presence of God not in the mind, but in the heart — a warmth, a light, or a profound sense of love.

- **Christ consciousness** is the idea of awakening to divine love as a living reality within. It goes beyond doctrine into direct experience — feeling the heart as the home of compassion, forgiveness, and grace.
- Mystics such as Meister Eckhart and St. Teresa of Ávila described the heart as a sanctuary where the soul meets God.
- In practice, this consciousness is lived through unconditional love, acts of service, and a willingness to see the divine spark in all beings.

Here we see a strong resonance with the Heart Chakra's role: the place where human love and divine love meet.

KABBALAH'S TIFERET: HARMONY AT THE CENTER

In Jewish mysticism, the Tree of Life maps ten sephirot, or spheres of divine qualities. At its center lies **Tiferet,** often translated as *beauty, harmony, or compassion.*

- Tiferet balances the higher and lower spheres, just as Anahata bridges the upper and lower chakras.
- It is associated with the heart, symbolizing integration, balance, and the beauty that arises when opposites unite.
- Tiferet is seen as the place where divine energy flows into the human soul, radiating love, balance, and truth.

Mystics saw Tiferet as the sephirah that harmonizes all others — much like the Heart Chakra harmonizes the human energy field.

A UNIVERSAL HEART

Though the symbols differ — a lotus in India, Christ in the heart, a shining sephirah in Kabbalah — the wisdom is the same: the heart is the center of balance, compassion, and divine connection.

In these teachings, the heart is not only where love is felt, but where heaven and earth meet. Whether through Christ consciousness, Tiferet, or Anahata, the message is clear: **awakening the heart is the path to awakening the soul.**

Chapter 8 – Balancing & Healing Practices

Reiki Positions and Energy Protocols for the Heart Chakra

In Reiki and other energy-healing systems, the hands act as conduits for universal life force energy. The Heart Chakra, located at the center of the chest, responds beautifully to this flow. By using specific hand positions and protocols, you can gently restore balance, clear blocks, and invite harmony back into Anahata.

HAND POSITIONS FOR SELF-TREATMENT

When working on your own heart, use these simple placements:

1. **Front of the Chest:** Place one or both hands over the sternum, fingers relaxed, palms resting gently on your body. This position directs Reiki energy into the front opening of the Heart Chakra.
2. **Back of the Heart:** Place one hand between your shoulder blades (or ask a practitioner to place theirs if you're receiving treatment). This connects to the back opening of the chakra, which often holds repressed emotions.
3. **Front and Back Together:** If possible, place one hand on the sternum and the other on the back of the chest at the same time. This creates a "sandwich" of energy, sending Reiki through the entire heart field.

Stay in each position for 3–5 minutes, or longer if you feel warmth, pulsing, or release.

PROTOCOLS FOR PRACTITIONERS

When treating others, Reiki practitioners often follow a sequence:

- **Start with grounding:** Place hands on the shoulders, hips, or feet to help the client feel safe and supported.
- **Move to the heart:** Place one hand on the sternum and the other beneath the upper back, allowing energy to flow through the chest.
- **Expand into the aura:** After working on the physical body, hover your hands a few inches above the chest, sensing the energy field. This can reveal imbalances like heaviness, heat, or cool spots.
- **Seal with balance:** Finish by holding both hands lightly over the sternum, imagining green (and/or pink) light radiating through the chest and into the aura.

ENERGETIC PROTOCOLS FOR HEART HEALING

Beyond simple placements, practitioners may use specific protocols:

- **Clearing Grief:** Gently sweep your hands upward from the chest into the air, as though lifting heavy energy out of the heart space. Replace it by holding your palms over the heart and imagining fresh light flowing in.
- **Restoring Balance:** Alternate your hands between the front and back of the heart, balancing giving (front) with receiving (back).
- **Heart Expansion:** Place both hands over the chest, then slowly move them outward while visualizing the aura expanding with light. This helps open the heart after contraction.

- **Integrating Love:** End by resting your hands in prayer position over the sternum, inviting both practitioner and client to silently affirm: *"I am love. I am loved. I radiate love."*

- **Trust your hands.** You may feel warmth, tingling, coolness, or pulsing — all signs of energy movement.
- **Listen to the client's body.** Some may sigh, cry, or breathe more deeply — natural releases of heart energy.
- **Always center yourself.** Begin each session by breathing into your own heart so you transmit Reiki with compassion, not sympathy or personal emotion.

Meditation & Visualization Exercises for the Heart Chakra

Working with Anahata doesn't require complex rituals — even simple meditations can open the heart gently and powerfully. Below are two classic practices you can return to anytime you wish to restore balance, release heaviness, or simply reconnect with love.

Green Light Meditation

The traditional color of the Heart Chakra is green — the color of balance, harmony, and renewal. Visualizing this light in your chest helps awaken healing energy and restore flow.

Steps:

1. Sit comfortably and close your eyes. Place one or both hands over your heart.

2. Take a few deep breaths, letting your chest expand and soften.
3. Imagine a soft green light glowing at the center of your sternum. With each breath in, the light grows brighter. With each breath out, it radiates further into your body.
4. See the light spreading through your chest, filling your lungs, and expanding into your entire aura.
5. Stay here for 5–10 minutes, breathing in love and breathing out peace.

Intention: *"My heart is open. I am balanced. I am love."*

Rose Meditation

Roses, especially pink and red, have long been linked with the heart. In this visualization, the rose becomes a living symbol of love unfolding within you.

Steps:

1. Sit quietly and place your hands in your lap, palms up.
2. Imagine a rosebud at the center of your chest. See its petals closed, holding the essence of love deep inside.
3. With each breath, the rose slowly begins to open — petal by petal.
4. As it blossoms, notice its color: perhaps soft pink for unconditional love, or deep red for passion, or green for balance.
5. Feel the fragrance of the rose radiating through your being, filling you with tenderness and warmth.
6. When the rose is fully open, imagine it sending love outward in all directions — to yourself, to loved ones, and to the world.

Intention: *"Like this rose, my heart opens with grace, beauty, and love."*

Meditation on the Twelve Petals of the Heart

Find a quiet space. Sit comfortably with your spine tall and your hands resting gently over your heart. Close your eyes. Take three deep, slow breaths. With each inhale, imagine green light filling your chest. With each exhale, imagine tension dissolving. Now, begin to visualize a lotus flower at the center of your chest, resting on your sternum. Its petals are closed, waiting to open.

The Unfolding

Petal 1: Joy
See the first petal slowly open, glowing with golden-green light. Feel joy bubbling up, not tied to anything outside you — just the natural joy of being alive. Whisper silently: *"Joy is my nature."*

Petal 2: Peace
The second petal unfurls. A calm, soft green light radiates outward, like still water. Feel peace settling into your breath, into your bones. *"Peace flows through me."*

Petal 3: Clarity
The third petal opens. Light becomes clear and bright, like sunlight after clouds. Confusion lifts. *"I see with the heart's wisdom."*

Petal 4: Love
The fourth petal glows brighter, radiating unconditional love. Not romantic, not possessive — but the love that simply is. *"I am love itself."*

Petal 5: Patience
The fifth petal stretches wide. Time slows. You feel no need to rush or force. *"I trust the unfolding."*

Petal 6: Kindness
The sixth petal opens, and you see gentle light touching everyone around you. Your heart smiles. *"Kindness flows through my hands, my words, my being."*

Petal 7: Understanding
The seventh petal reveals itself. You feel empathy deepening into wisdom. You understand yourself and others without judgment. *"I listen with the heart."*

Petal 8: Harmony
The eighth petal radiates like music. Your breath, your body, your energy align. *"I live in harmony with myself, with others, with life."*

Petal 9: Empathy
The ninth petal glows warmly. You feel connected, able to sense another's feelings while staying steady within yourself. *"I feel with others, without losing myself."*

Petal 10: Compassion
The tenth petal opens wide. Compassion pours out like a river. *"My love brings healing to all beings."*

Petal 11: Forgiveness
The eleventh petal glows like soft fire, dissolving old wounds. You feel the chains of the past fall away. *"I forgive. I release. I am free."*

Petal 12: Bliss
The final petal blossoms fully. Your chest glows with radiant green light, merging into gold, pink, and white. You feel joy, peace, and love all at once. *"I am one with all. I am bliss."*

Integration

See the lotus fully open now, twelve petals shining in perfect balance. Its light extends beyond your body, filling the room, connecting you to all of life. Sit in this radiance for a few breaths.

When you are ready, bring your hands together at your heart in gratitude. Whisper: *"May my heart remain open. May I live these petals of love."*

Take three deep breaths. Gently open your eyes, carrying this heart light into your day.

Why These Practices Work

- **Visualization** engages the mind and body together, creating real shifts in the energy field.
- **Color and symbol** (green light, rose) speak directly to the subconscious and help unlock stored emotions.
- **Breath awareness** naturally calms the nervous system, allowing the heart to soften and expand.

Sound Healing for the Heart Chakra

The Heart Chakra responds powerfully to vibration. Whether through mantra, instruments, or music, sound can bypass the thinking mind and speak directly to the energy of Anahata. These practices use resonance to dissolve blockages, restore flow, and expand love.

The YAM Mantra

Every chakra has a seed sound, or *bija mantra.* For the Heart Chakra, that sound is **YAM** (pronounced "yahm"). Chanting it creates a vibration that resonates through the chest, loosening heaviness and awakening compassion.

Practice:

1. Sit comfortably, hands over your heart.
2. Take a deep breath in, and as you exhale, chant slowly: "Yaaaaam."
3. Feel the vibration echo in your sternum and ribs.
4. Repeat for several minutes, letting the sound soften and expand the energy of the heart.

Tip: Try chanting with a group. The shared vibration magnifies the opening of collective heart energy.

Tuning Forks and Frequency Healing

The Heart Chakra is often associated with frequencies like **639 Hz** — a tone linked with love, harmony, and connection. Practitioners of sound therapy use tuning forks or singing bowls tuned to this frequency to rebalance Anahata.

Practice:

- Strike a 639 Hz tuning fork and place its base gently on the sternum, letting the vibration travel into the chest.
- Move the fork slowly through the aura around your heart, noticing shifts in sensation.
- If you use a singing bowl, place it in front of the chest and allow its resonance to wash over you.

Even without tools, simply listening to music tuned to 639 Hz can have a calming, heart-opening effect.

Heart-Opening Music

Not all sound healing has to be technical. Music itself is medicine for the heart. Gentle melodies, harmonies, and rhythms can unlock emotions, soothe grief, and inspire joy.

Suggestions:

- Listen to soft flute, harp, or piano music when meditating on Anahata.
- Choose chants, kirtan, or sacred music that center on love and devotion.
- Allow yourself to sing — even quietly. Your own voice is one of the most healing vibrations for your heart.

Why Sound Works

Sound is vibration, and vibration is energy. By directing sound into the chest — through mantra, frequency, or music — you invite the Heart Chakra to resonate with its natural harmony. Over time, this resonance dissolves blockages and restores the heart's true rhythm: openness, balance, and love.

Crystals for the Heart Chakra

Crystals carry unique vibrations that can amplify and support the healing of Anahata. The Heart Chakra resonates especially with stones in shades of **green and pink** — each offering different facets of love, balance, and harmony.

ROSE QUARTZ – THE STONE OF UNCONDITIONAL LOVE

Perhaps the most well-known heart crystal, rose quartz radiates gentle, nurturing energy. It encourages self-love, softens grief, and opens the heart to giving and receiving affection.

How to use it:

- Place over your sternum during meditation to soothe emotional wounds.
- Carry in your pocket to remind yourself of compassion throughout the day.
- Sleep with it under your pillow to invite loving dreams and emotional release.

EMERALD – THE STONE OF HARMONY AND ABUNDANCE

Emerald is traditionally associated with prosperity, truth, and emotional balance. It strengthens relationships, deepens trust, and aligns the heart with integrity.

How to use it:

- Wear as jewelry over the chest to promote honesty and harmony in relationships.
- Meditate with emerald when seeking clarity in matters of love or forgiveness.
- Place it in shared spaces to create a field of peace and balance.

JADE – THE STONE OF PEACE AND PROTECTION

Green jade has been revered in many cultures as a stone of protection, luck, and long life. For the heart, it brings calmness, stabilizes emotions, and helps release fear.

How to use it:

- Hold during breathwork to settle anxiety and bring balance.
- Use in massage tools (gua sha or rollers) over the chest and face to move stagnant energy.

- Gift jade to loved ones as a token of enduring friendship and connection.

OTHER HELPFUL HEART STONES

- **Malachite:** Deep healing, transformation, breaking old patterns of pain.
- **Green Aventurine:** Optimism, growth, and renewed confidence in love.
- **Pink Tourmaline:** Emotional release, comfort during heartbreak.
- **Rhodochrosite:** Self-compassion and healing of inner child wounds.

SIMPLE CRYSTAL PRACTICES

- **Heart Layout:** Lie down and place one green stone (like jade or emerald) and one pink stone (like rose quartz) over your chest. Breathe deeply, imagining the colors weaving together in your heart.
- **Crystal Elixir:** Place cleansed stones (safe for water, e.g., rose quartz, jade, aventurine) in a glass of water overnight. Drink in the morning to "absorb" their vibration.
- **Daily Reminder:** Carry a pocket stone and touch it whenever you feel your heart closing — a simple anchor to bring you back to love.

WHY CRYSTALS WORK FOR THE HEART

Crystals act as tuning forks for your energy field. Just as sound aligns vibration, crystals radiate steady frequencies that help guide the Heart Chakra back to balance. Green stones restore harmony and growth; pink stones encourage tenderness and unconditional love. Together, they create a complete spectrum of heart healing.

Essential Oils for the Heart Chakra

The Heart Chakra responds beautifully to aroma because scent is directly linked to memory, emotion, and mood. Using essential oils in meditation, massage, or daily rituals can open the chest, soothe heavy emotions, and encourage balance. Oils connected with **flowers, citrus, and light woods** are especially supportive for Anahata.

Rose – The Oil of Unconditional Love

Known as the "queen of oils," rose has the highest vibrational frequency of all essential oils. Its scent is soft, floral, and deeply nurturing. Rose oil opens the heart, heals grief, and encourages unconditional self-love.
Use: Place a drop over your heart (diluted in carrier oil), inhale during meditation, or diffuse in your space.

Geranium – The Oil of Emotional Balance

Geranium harmonizes the nervous system and balances emotions. It lifts heavy moods, soothes anger, and helps restore trust in relationships.
Use: Add to a warm bath, mix into massage oil, or diffuse when working through emotional stress.

Bergamot – The Oil of Joy and Lightness

Bergamot, a citrus oil, brightens the spirit and eases tension in the chest. It is especially helpful for releasing anxiety, self-doubt, or fear of rejection.
Use: Diffuse in the morning to invite optimism, or apply (diluted) to pulse points before heart-centered practices.

Other Helpful Oils for the Heart

- **Lavender:** Calms grief and soothes emotional pain.
- **Ylang-Ylang:** Awakens sensuality and helps release jealousy or over-attachment.
- **Eucalyptus:** Clears stagnation in the lungs, supporting both breath and heart flow.
- **Sandalwood:** Encourages spiritual connection and inner peace.
- **Marjoram:** Softens loneliness and feelings of isolation.

SIMPLE PRACTICES

- **Heart Anointing:** Place a drop of rose or geranium oil (with carrier oil) directly over your sternum. Breathe deeply, visualizing green or pink light radiating outward.
- **Aromatic Breathing:** Put 1–2 drops of oil on a tissue, hold it near your nose, and breathe into the heart space for 1–2 minutes.
- **Diffuser Ritual:** Diffuse a heart blend (rose, bergamot, lavender) while meditating, journaling, or practicing Reiki.
- **Self-Massage:** Combine a heart oil with a carrier oil (like jojoba or almond) and gently massage the chest, shoulders, and upper back to open circulation and release tension.

WHY OILS WORK FOR THE HEART

Essential oils are more than pleasant scents — they are concentrated plant essences with energetic properties. For the Heart Chakra, oils that are floral (love), citrus (joy), and woodsy (grounded peace) provide the perfect spectrum of healing. Used regularly, they gently dissolve blocks, calm the mind, and invite love to flow freely.

Somatic Practices for the Heart Chakra

The Heart Chakra is not only an energy center — it's also housed in the body. Stress, grief, and emotional tension often show up as tightness in the chest, shallow breathing, or hunched shoulders. Somatic practices use simple physical movements and touch to **release tension and invite openness**, making space for love and balance to flow more freely.

Chest Opening Stretches

- **Why it works:** When the chest muscles are tight, the heart center feels physically closed. Stretching creates space in the sternum and lungs, signaling safety to the nervous system.
- **Practice:**
  1. Stand tall and clasp your hands behind your back.
  2. Roll your shoulders back and gently lift your chest upward.
  3. Take 5 slow breaths, imagining green light expanding from your sternum.
- **Variation:** Lie on the floor with a pillow or bolster under your upper back, arms wide, chest lifted. Breathe deeply into your heart space.

Sternum Tapping

- **Why it works:** Gentle tapping on the sternum stimulates the thymus gland, which supports immunity and is linked with heart energy. It also helps break up stagnation in the chest.
- **Practice:**
  1. Using your fingertips, gently tap the center of your chest in a steady rhythm.

2. While tapping, breathe deeply and repeat an affirmation such as *"I open my heart to love."*
3. Continue for 1–2 minutes until you feel warmth, tingling, or emotional release.

Heart-Soothing Touch

- **Why it works:** The body responds to nurturing touch, even from yourself. Placing your hands on your chest signals comfort and helps calm the nervous system.
- **Practice:**
   1. Place one hand over your heart, the other over your solar plexus.
   2. Breathe slowly, imagining your hands radiating warmth inward.
   3. Whisper kind words to yourself, like *"I am safe. I am loved."*

Dynamic Shake & Release

- **Why it works:** Unexpressed emotions often get "stuck" in the body. Gentle shaking loosens tension, allowing the heart space to feel lighter.
- **Practice:**
   1. Stand with feet hip-width apart.
   2. Shake your arms, shoulders, and chest gently for 30–60 seconds.
   3. Let out a sigh or sound on the exhale to release emotional residue.

The Gift of Somatic Practice

These movements may seem simple, but they unlock deep shifts. By working directly with the body, you help the heart feel safe to open. Over time, these practices retrain the nervous system to respond to stress with resilience and to life with love.

Yoga and Breathwork for the Heart Chakra

The Heart Chakra is deeply connected to breath and posture. When the chest is tight or the breath is shallow, energy in Anahata becomes constricted. Yoga and breathwork (pranayama) help expand the chest, soften the spine, and circulate prana (life force), creating space for love and compassion to flow.

YOGA POSES FOR ANAHATA

Heart-opening poses gently stretch the chest and shoulders while inviting courage and vulnerability.

- **Camel Pose (Ustrasana):** A deep backbend that expands the chest and stretches the front body, helping release stored grief or fear.
- **Bridge Pose (Setu Bandhasana):** Lifts the heart upward, energizing the chest and calming the nervous system.
- **Cobra Pose (Bhujangasana):** Strengthens the spine while gently opening the chest, encouraging confidence and warmth.
- **Upward-Facing Dog (Urdhva Mukha Svanasana):** Invigorates the lungs, expands the heart space, and builds resilience.
- **Supported Fish Pose (Matsyasana with props):** A gentle restorative pose that passively opens the chest and soothes the heart.
- **Child's Pose with Arms Extended (Balasana variation):** Brings grounding while subtly stretching the chest, reminding the heart to soften.

Practice Tip: In every heart-opener, keep the focus on lifting and expanding the chest, not collapsing the lower back. Imagine breathing directly into the center of your sternum.

BREATHWORK PRACTICES

1. Heart-Centered Breathing

- Sit comfortably, one hand on your heart.
- Inhale deeply, imagining breath flowing directly into the chest.
- Exhale slowly, visualizing green or pink light expanding outward.
- Repeat for 5–10 minutes to calm the nervous system and reconnect with compassion.

2. Alternate Nostril Breathing (Nadi Shodhana)
This pranayama balances energy channels, calming the mind and harmonizing the heart.

- Use the thumb to close one nostril, inhale through the other.
- Switch, exhaling through the opposite nostril, then inhaling.
- Continue alternating for several minutes, focusing on balance and inner peace.

3. Breath of Gratitude

- With each inhale, silently say: *"I receive love."*
- With each exhale, silently say: *"I give love."*
- Continue for 3–5 minutes, allowing gratitude to expand with every breath.

4. Sighing Breath (Clearing Release)

- Inhale deeply through the nose.
- Exhale with an audible sigh through the mouth.
- Repeat several times to release tension, grief, or heaviness in the chest.

WHY YOGA AND BREATHWORK WORK FOR THE HEART

These practices create both physical and energetic expansion. The poses open the ribcage and lungs, releasing trapped energy, while the breath circulates prana through Anahata. Together, they soften defenses, calm the mind, and restore the heart's natural rhythm of openness and love.

Food Therapy for the Heart Chakra

What you eat doesn't just nourish your body — it also affects your energy. The Heart Chakra resonates with foods that are light, fresh, and high in vitality. Choosing heart-friendly meals can strengthen both the physical heart and the energetic field of Anahata.

Leafy Greens: The Core of Heart Healing

Because the Heart Chakra is traditionally green, foods in this color family bring natural balance and restoration. Leafy greens are especially powerful because they carry chlorophyll — a plant compound that helps oxygenate and energize the body.

- **Examples:** spinach, kale, arugula, collard greens, romaine, bok choy, parsley.
- **Benefits:** cleanse the blood, support circulation, and provide magnesium and iron for a calm, steady heartbeat.
- **Energy effect:** green foods harmonize the aura, encourage balance, and connect you to the energy of growth and renewal.

High-Vibration Fruits & Vegetables

Fresh, raw, and colorful produce carries a high life-force energy that lifts the spirit. For Anahata, choose foods that are not only green, but also those linked with lightness and heart health.

- **Examples:** cucumbers, zucchini, avocado, green apples, pears, kiwis, limes.
- **Benefits:** hydrate the body, improve digestion, and support healthy cholesterol levels.
- **Energy effect:** encourage openness and flow, releasing heaviness from the heart space.

Heart-Healing Herbs & Teas

Herbs have long been used to soothe both the heart and lungs, the two organs connected with Anahata.

- **Hawthorn:** strengthens the physical heart and balances blood pressure.
- **Rose petals:** softens grief and opens emotional expression.
- **Tulsi (Holy Basil):** calms stress and restores spiritual clarity.
- **Mint:** refreshes the breath and opens the lungs, clearing the chest area.

Foods that Radiate Love Energy

Beyond greens, certain foods are associated with tenderness and self-care — they "feel good" as well as nourish.

- **Dark chocolate (in moderation):** improves circulation and stimulates serotonin, the "feel-good" hormone.
- **Raw honey:** natural sweetness that uplifts the mood.
- **Nuts and seeds (especially pumpkin and sunflower):** provide grounding while still supporting heart energy.

What to Minimize

Just as some foods uplift the heart, others weigh it down energetically. Heavy, processed, or overly greasy foods can dull the energy field. Excess caffeine or sugar may overstimulate the heart, creating anxiety or jitteriness.

Practical Rituals for Heart Food Therapy

- **Eat mindfully:** Bless your food with gratitude before eating, imagining it filling your heart with love.
- **Color therapy on your plate:** Add something green to every meal as a daily heart practice.
- **Infuse love into preparation:** Cooking with care — even chopping herbs with presence — transfers loving energy into your food.

Why Food Matters for Anahata

Food carries vibration. When you eat fresh, living foods — especially leafy greens and heart-healing herbs — you're not just feeding your body, but tuning your heart to balance, renewal, and love.

Experience the Heart in Action

Reading about the Heart Chakra is powerful — but sometimes the heart needs to *move*. To help you embody what you've learned, I invite you to join me in a guided **Heart Chakra Meditation** on YouTube. In the video, I walk you step-by-step through opening, clearing, and connecting with Anahata.

You can watch it here: https://youtu.be/QE5r30Q65gg

Feel free to pause, return, or replay parts as often as you like. Let this meditation be your companion on the path to an open, balanced heart.

Nature Practices for the Heart Chakra

The Heart Chakra is naturally attuned to the rhythms of nature. Its color is green, the same energy that fills forests, fields, and plants with life. When you spend time in nature, you're not just relaxing — you're **aligning your heart field with the Earth's field.**

WALKING MEDITATIONS IN FORESTS

- **Why it works:** Forests radiate the frequency of green, which resonates with the heart's energy of balance and renewal. Each breath of fresh air oxygenates your body and calms your nervous system, while the rhythm of walking grounds your energy.
- **How to do it:**
    1. Choose a natural space — a forest, park, or even a tree-lined path.
    2. Walk slowly and mindfully, feeling each step connect to the earth.
    3. With every inhale, imagine drawing green light from the trees into your chest.
    4. With every exhale, imagine your heart releasing gratitude back into the earth.
- **The effect:** Your heart begins to synchronize with the living pulse of the forest, creating inner calm and connection.

HEART ATTUNEMENT WITH PLANTS OR TREES

- **Why it works:** Plants, especially trees, are living beings with their own energy fields. Sitting with them allows your heart chakra to resonate with their steady, nurturing vibration.
- **How to do it:**

1. Find a tree that feels inviting. Sit or stand near it, placing your hands over your heart.
2. Close your eyes and breathe slowly, imagining your heart connecting with the tree's heartwood.
3. If comfortable, place a hand on the tree trunk. Feel its strength and rootedness flowing into your body.
4. Silently say: *"May our hearts beat as one in balance and love."*

- **The effect:** Many people report feeling calmer, lighter, or embraced by the presence of the tree. This is heart-to-heart resonance with the natural world.

DAILY GREEN CONNECTION

Even if you can't reach a forest, you can invite Anahata's resonance into your day:

- Keep plants in your home or workspace.
- Drink herbal teas with green leaves (mint, tulsi, green tea).
- Step outside to place your bare feet on the grass and breathe deeply.

THE GIFT OF NATURE PRACTICES

Nature reminds us that love is not just human — it is universal. By attuning your heart to the green life force around you, you reconnect with balance, compassion, and the truth that you are part of a greater whole.

Chapter 9 – Advanced Practitioner Applications

Using Heart Energy as a Gateway to Intuitive Healing

For energy practitioners, the Heart Chakra is more than just a center of compassion — it is a **gateway.** When Anahata is open, balanced, and radiating, it allows the healer to connect with intuition in a way that feels clear, grounded, and trustworthy. This is why many traditions teach that the heart, not the mind, should guide healing work.

WHY THE HEART IS THE GATEWAY

- **Neutrality:** The heart field is expansive and inclusive. Unlike the mind, which may judge or doubt, the heart perceives without distortion.
- **Connection:** The electromagnetic field of the heart is many times stronger than that of the brain. When open, it creates resonance between practitioner and client.
- **Integration:** The heart bridges body and spirit, making intuitive insights both spiritually guided and practically grounded.

When you approach healing from the heart, intuition becomes less about "trying to figure things out" and more about *allowing awareness to arise naturally.*

PRACTICAL APPLICATION FOR PRACTITIONERS

1. Centering in the Heart
Before beginning any session, place your hands over your own chest. Breathe deeply until you feel warmth or expansion. Silently affirm:
"I open my heart as a clear channel for love and truth."
This aligns your intuitive field before you connect with your client.

2. Sensing Through the Heart Field
Instead of scanning with the mind, let your awareness rest in the heart. As you move your hands through the aura or place them on the body, notice:

- Subtle shifts in temperature.
- Emotional impressions or images.
- A pull, push, or tingling sensation in your chest that mirrors your client's imbalance.

This is intuition flowing through resonance.

3. Heart-Led Guidance
When insights arise (a word, image, or inner knowing), check them against your heart. Ask inwardly: *"Does this feel expansive, compassionate, and true?"* If the answer is yes, it is guidance. If the answer contracts or feels heavy, it may be a projection from the mind.

EXAMPLE IN PRACTICE

A Reiki practitioner begins a session. Instead of trying to "see" imbalances with the third eye, they soften into the heart space. As they hover their hands above the chest, they feel a wave of grief, mirrored by a heaviness in their own sternum. Trusting the heart, they place both hands gently over the client's chest.

The client later shares they had been holding unresolved sadness — confirming the intuitive insight.

Using the heart as a gateway transforms healing from a technical practice into a sacred connection. Clients don't just feel treated — they feel *seen, held, and understood.* This is the difference between doing Reiki as a technique and embodying Reiki as a way of being.

Heart Energy and Hands-On Healing Protocols for Practitioners

Working with the Heart Chakra in a healing session requires more than technique — it requires presence. These step-by-step protocols combine Reiki hand placements with intentional heart energy, so practitioners can create a safe and deeply transformative experience.

Step 1: Center Yourself in the Heart

Before beginning with a client:

1. Place both hands over your own chest.
2. Breathe slowly into your sternum, feeling warmth or expansion.
3. Silently affirm: *"I am a clear and loving channel for healing energy."*
   This ensures you are anchored in compassion and not projecting personal emotion.

Step 2: Prepare the Client

- Invite them to lie comfortably on a massage table or sit in a supportive chair.
- Encourage them to close their eyes and place one hand over their own chest if it feels natural — this creates an immediate connection with Anahata.
- Ask them to set a simple intention, such as: *"I open my heart to balance and healing."*

Step 3: Core Heart Positions

The **front and back of the chest** are the primary placements:

1. Place one hand gently over the sternum (front heart center).
2. Place the other hand between the shoulder blades (back heart center).
    - If this is not physically possible, alternate hands between front and back.
    - This "sandwich" of energy connects both openings of the chakra, often bringing profound release.

Hold for 3–5 minutes, or longer if you sense pulsing, warmth, or emotional shifts.

Step 4: Aura Clearing Around the Heart

- Hover your hands 2–6 inches above the chest.
- Slowly move them in small circles or sweeping motions, noticing areas of heaviness, heat, or coolness.
- Imagine drawing out stagnant energy with each sweep, then shaking or brushing it away.
- Replace it by visualizing green or pink light flowing through your palms into the client's heart field.

Step 5: Heart Expansion Protocol

1. Place both hands over the sternum.
2. After a few breaths, slowly move your hands outward to the sides, as if opening a curtain.
3. Visualize the chest filling with light that expands beyond the body.
   This helps restore trust, openness, and resilience after contraction or grief.

Step 6: Integration and Closing

- Return your hands to the sternum, holding gently until you feel balance and calm.
- Invite the client to take three deep breaths, imagining their chest glowing with radiant green or pink light.
- Seal the session by silently affirming: *"May this heart remain open, balanced, and strong."*

Tips for Practitioners

- **Stay present.** Clients can feel the difference between mechanical hand placement and heart-centered presence.
- **Honor emotion.** Tears, sighs, or even laughter are signs of release. Allow them without judgment.
- **Ground afterward.** Always finish with grounding (hands on feet, hips, or shoulders) to help the client integrate the heart opening into daily life.

THE PRACTITIONER'S EXPERIENCE

When you work with the Heart Chakra in this way, you may notice sensations in your own chest — warmth, tingling, or a sudden flood of compassion. This is not a distraction but a sign of resonance: your heart field and your client's heart field are aligning.

The Role of Anahata in Distant / Remote Healing

One of the most profound aspects of energy healing is that it is **not bound by space or time.** Practitioners of Reiki, prayer, and other energy traditions have long reported that healing can be sent across miles — sometimes even across generations. At the core of this ability lies the **Heart Chakra.**

WHY THE HEART IS THE CONDUIT

- **Resonance Field:** Science shows that the electromagnetic field of the heart extends several feet beyond the body. In energy traditions, this field is seen as limitless — capable of reaching and resonating with another person's energy no matter where they are.
- **Connection Beyond Mind:** While the mind may question distance, the heart knows connection. When a practitioner anchors in Anahata, they access the natural truth that love and compassion are not limited by geography.
- **Safety and Clarity:** Remote healing sent through the heart is less likely to carry ego or personal agenda. It flows with compassion, ensuring the energy arrives where it is needed in the right way.

HOW PRACTITIONERS USE THE HEART IN DISTANT HEALING

1. **Center in Your Own Heart** – Place your hands over your chest and breathe until you feel warmth or expansion.
2. **Visualize Connection** – Imagine a thread of green or pink light extending from your heart to the heart of the person you are sending healing to.

3. **Channel Reiki / Energy** – Place your hands in a heart-focused position (palms together or over your chest) and intend that the universal life force flows through your heart and outward.
4. **Trust the Bridge** – Instead of trying to control where the energy goes, trust that the heart knows the path.

EXAMPLE PROTOCOL

- Begin by calling the person's name silently.
- See them surrounded by a field of soft green light.
- Imagine your own heart lotus opening, sending petals of light across the distance.
- Hold this vision for several minutes, silently affirming: *"May your heart be at peace. May you be balanced. May you be loved."*
- When complete, gently release the connection and ground yourself.

CLIENT EXPERIENCE

Recipients of distant healing often report:

- Feeling sudden warmth or tingling in the chest.
- Experiencing calm, tears, or emotional release.
- Sensing a supportive presence, as though someone is holding them with love.

These responses mirror in-person heart-centered healing, showing that distance is not a barrier when the heart is the medium.

THE HIDDEN GIFT

Anahata makes distant healing possible because it embodies **oneness.** When you open your heart, you step beyond the illusion of separation. Sending Reiki or prayer through the heart is not about projecting energy outward, but about *remembering connection* — that you and the other are already joined in the field of love.

Clearing Ancestral Grief and Karmic Imprints

The Heart Chakra doesn't only carry your personal joys and sorrows. It also holds the **echoes of those who came before you.** Family grief, unhealed traumas, and even karmic patterns from previous lifetimes can settle in the heart field, shaping how you experience love, trust, and connection.

Far from being a burden, these imprints are an invitation: when cleared, they free not only you, but also your lineage — past, present, and future.

HOW ANCESTRAL GRIEF LIVES IN THE HEART

- **Inherited Emotion:** You may feel grief that does not match your life story — sadness without a clear cause, or a heaviness in the chest that has no obvious trigger.
- **Family Beliefs:** Messages like "love always hurts" or "we don't talk about feelings" are subtle imprints that close the heart.
- **Repeated Patterns:** Generational cycles of betrayal, abandonment, or emotional numbness often leave their mark in Anahata.

KARMIC IMPRINTS

In yogic and esoteric traditions, the heart is considered the seat of the soul. This means unresolved lessons from past lives may surface here as:

- Fear of intimacy without a clear reason.
- A tendency to sabotage love.
- An unshakable sense of loss or guilt that feels older than this lifetime.

These karmic threads aren't punishment — they are opportunities for healing and integration.

HEART-CENTERED CLEARING PRACTICE (FOR PRACTITIONERS)

1. **Prepare:** Center yourself in your own heart field with a few deep breaths.
2. **Invite Ancestral Presence:** Silently affirm, *"I welcome the love of my ancestors, and I release what no longer serves."*
3. **Connect:** Place hands over the client's sternum and upper back. Sense if there is heaviness, density, or lingering grief.
4. **Visualize Clearing:** Imagine green light radiating from your palms, dissolving gray or heavy patterns in the chest.
5. **Release:** Sweep your hands upward and outward, symbolically lifting grief from the heart field.
6. **Replace:** Visualize a pink or emerald light filling the space, anchoring in love and renewal.

INTEGRATION

Encourage the client to:

- Journal about family patterns of love and loss.
- Create rituals of release (lighting a candle for ancestors, saying prayers of forgiveness, or offering flowers).
- Practice daily heart affirmations such as: *"I carry forward love, not sorrow. I choose connection, not fear."*

THE HIDDEN GIFT

Clearing ancestral grief and karmic imprints through the heart doesn't erase history — it transforms it. The Heart Chakra has the power to turn inherited wounds into compassion, karmic burdens into wisdom, and grief into resilience.

By doing this work, you become a **heart-keeper** for your lineage — breaking cycles of pain and opening pathways of love for generations to come.

Cross-Referencing with TCM Meridians: Lung and Heart

Although chakras come from the yogic and Tantric traditions of India, their principles often echo those found in other healing systems. In **Traditional Chinese Medicine (TCM),** energy flows through meridians — channels that nourish the body, mind, and spirit. Interestingly, the Heart Chakra aligns closely with the **heart and lung meridians** in TCM, creating fascinating points of connection.

THE HEART MERIDIAN

In TCM, the heart is called the **"Emperor"** — the ruler that governs spirit (Shen), joy, and emotional clarity. When the heart meridian is in balance:

- Emotions flow freely.
- Speech is clear and compassionate.
- The spirit feels calm and radiant.

Signs of imbalance mirror those of Anahata: anxiety, restlessness, bitterness, or even chest pain.

Overlap with Heart Chakra: Both view the heart as more than a physical organ — it is the seat of consciousness, love, and spiritual presence.

THE LUNG MERIDIAN

The lungs in TCM are linked with **breath, grief, and letting go.** They draw in vital Qi (life force) and release what no longer serves.

When the lung meridian is balanced:

- Breathing is smooth and nourishing.
- Grief is acknowledged and released.
- The immune system is strong.

Signs of imbalance: shortness of breath, chronic sadness, weak immunity, or difficulty releasing the past.

Overlap with Heart Chakra: The Heart Chakra is often where grief is carried. Just as the lungs help us exhale what we no longer need, Anahata helps us emotionally release old pain and loss.

THE HEART–LUNG CONNECTION

In TCM, the heart and lungs are deeply interdependent:

- The heart governs blood circulation.
- The lungs govern Qi (breath) circulation.
  Together, they ensure the flow of life force through the body.

In the chakra system, Anahata also sits at the crossroads of breath and circulation — symbolically and physically connecting love, vitality, and compassion.

PRACTICAL INTEGRATION FOR PRACTITIONERS

- **Reiki + Acupressure:** When treating the Heart Chakra, place hands over the chest while gently pressing Lung 1 (LU-1, Zhongfu, just under the collarbone) or Heart 7 (HT-7, Shenmen, at the wrist crease) to harmonize both systems.
- **Breath + Intention:** Use lung-focused breathing exercises to clear grief before heart-opening meditations.
- **Cross-System Awareness:** Notice that what TCM calls *Qi stagnation in the chest* often corresponds to what chakra practitioners describe as a *blocked Anahata.*

THE HIDDEN TRUTH

Though they arose in different cultures, both systems recognize the same wisdom: the heart and lungs are not just physical organs, but **gateways of love, breath, and spirit.** Whether you speak of meridians or chakras, the message is clear — healing the chest is healing the soul.

Heart Coherence Techniques: Linking Practitioner's and Client's Heart Rhythms

In both spiritual traditions and modern science, the heart is recognized as more than a pump. It has its own rhythm, intelligence, and electromagnetic field. When two people come together — especially in healing work — their heart fields can **synchronize.** This state is called **heart coherence.**

For practitioners, consciously cultivating coherence creates a safe, powerful space where healing flows more easily.

WHAT IS HEART COHERENCE?

- In scientific terms, heart coherence is a state where the heartbeat becomes smooth and rhythmic, aligning with breathing and emotional calm.
- In energetic terms, coherence occurs when the practitioner's heart field resonates with the client's, creating entrainment — the tendency of two rhythms to synchronize.
- In practice, this means the client begins to feel calmer, safer, and more open simply by being in the presence of a coherent heart field.

WHY IT MATTERS IN HEALING

- **Safety:** Clients can sense when a practitioner is centered versus distracted. Coherence creates trust.
- **Amplification:** A coherent heart field magnifies the effectiveness of Reiki or energy healing, allowing the client's system to entrain to balance more quickly.
- **Intuition:** When your heart is coherent, intuitive insights flow more clearly, without interference from mental chatter.

HOW TO CREATE HEART COHERENCE AS A PRACTITIONER

Step 1: Center Yourself

- Place your hands over your chest.
- Inhale slowly for 5 seconds, exhale slowly for 5 seconds.
- Imagine breathing directly through your heart.

Step 2: Cultivate a Heart Emotion

- Focus on a feeling of gratitude, compassion, or love.

- Let this emotion expand until you feel warmth in your chest.

Step 3: Extend the Field

- Imagine this rhythm radiating from your heart like waves.
- As you place your hands on or above the client, allow your heart rhythm to guide the session.

Step 4: Invite Resonance

- Without forcing, hold the intention: *"May our hearts find harmony in this moment of healing."*
- Notice subtle shifts — deeper breathing, softened expression, or relaxation in the client — as signs of entrainment.

HEART-TO-HEART PROTOCOL (ADVANCED)

1. Sit beside the client and place one hand gently over their sternum (with consent).
2. Place your other hand over your own heart.
3. Synchronize your breathing with theirs, gently lengthening the rhythm.
4. Visualize both hearts glowing in green light, pulsing together in harmony.
5. Hold for 2–3 minutes, then release slowly, allowing each heart to continue its natural rhythm.

THE HIDDEN GIFT

Heart coherence is not about control — it is about resonance. By embodying calm, gratitude, and compassion, practitioners allow clients to *feel safe enough to heal.* The true power of this technique lies not in the hands, but in the invisible harmony of two hearts beating in connection.

Integration with Modern Healing

Ancient traditions have long described the heart as a center of wisdom and energy. Today, science is beginning to confirm what healers have always known: the heart is not just a physical pump, but a powerful communication hub between body, mind, and spirit. By blending Heart Chakra practices with modern tools like biofeedback, HRV training, and heart-brain coherence research, practitioners can expand both their effectiveness and credibility.

BIOFEEDBACK AND THE HEART

- **What it is:** Biofeedback uses sensors to monitor physiological signals (like breathing, heart rate, or skin temperature) and gives real-time feedback.
- **How it connects to Anahata:** When clients see their stress patterns on a screen, they can practice relaxation techniques — including heart-centered breathing and affirmations — to shift into balance. Watching their own heart rhythm stabilize reinforces the power of the Heart Chakra.
- **Practical use:** Combine a short Reiki heart placement with guided breathing while the client watches their feedback screen — bridging energy practice with measurable results.

HEART RATE VARIABILITY (HRV) TRAINING

- **What it is:** HRV measures the variation in time between heartbeats. High HRV is linked to resilience, emotional regulation, and overall well-being. Low HRV often correlates with stress, anxiety, or burnout.
- **How it connects to Anahata:** Practices like slow breathing, gratitude meditation, and chanting directly

improve HRV. These are the same techniques ancient healers used to open the Heart Chakra.

- **Practical use:** Encourage clients to track HRV while doing heart-based practices (like inhaling green light or repeating "I am love"). This makes the invisible — the flow of heart energy — visible and empowering.

HEART-BRAIN COHERENCE (HEARTMATH INSTITUTE)

- **What it is:** Research from the *HeartMath Institute* shows that the heart and brain are in constant communication. When the heart is in coherence (a smooth, steady rhythm), the brain functions more clearly, emotions stabilize, and intuition heightens.
- **How it connects to Anahata:** In energy work, this is what we call heart-centered living — aligning thought, emotion, and spirit.
- **Practical use:** Before a healing session, both practitioner and client can practice HeartMath's "Quick Coherence Technique":
  1. Focus attention on the heart area.
  2. Breathe slowly and evenly through the heart.
  3. Recall a feeling of gratitude or love until the chest feels warm or expansive.

The Gift of Integration

By weaving together Reiki, meditation, and chakra practices with modern tools like HRV training and coherence monitoring, practitioners can validate ancient wisdom through science. This builds trust with clients, enhances measurable outcomes, and demonstrates that **love, compassion, and balance are not just "spiritual ideals," but physiological realities.**

Scientific Sidebar: HeartMath and the Science of Coherence

Modern research supports what healers have known for centuries: the heart is more than a physical organ — it is also an **information and communication center.**

- **The Heart's Electromagnetic Field:** Studies by the *HeartMath Institute* show that the heart produces the strongest electromagnetic field in the body — about 60 times greater in amplitude than the brain's electrical activity. This field can be measured several feet away from the body.
- **Coherence Defined:** When the heart's rhythm is smooth and ordered (often achieved through slow breathing and feelings like gratitude or love), the body enters a state called **heart coherence.** In this state, the heart, brain, and nervous system work in harmony.
- **Emotional Effects:** People in coherence report increased calm, emotional resilience, and clarity of thought. Their immune systems and hormonal balance also improve.
- **Shared Fields:** Perhaps most intriguing, HeartMath's research suggests that one person's coherent heart field can influence another's. This supports the ancient belief that healers can "hold space" for clients by radiating calm, loving energy.

In practice: By cultivating coherence before and during a session, practitioners don't just work on the client — they create a shared field where healing naturally unfolds.

Combining Heart Chakra Work with Hypnosis, Reflexology, or Aromatherapy

The Heart Chakra does not exist in isolation — it responds beautifully when paired with other healing methods. By blending Anahata practices with modalities like hypnosis, reflexology, and aromatherapy, practitioners can create **layered experiences** that deepen release, accelerate balance, and anchor heart healing into body, mind, and spirit.

HYPNOSIS AND THE HEART

Hypnosis works by guiding the client into a deeply relaxed, receptive state where the subconscious mind can shift patterns.

- **Why it works with Anahata:** The subconscious often stores unprocessed grief, fear of intimacy, or limiting beliefs about love. Pairing hypnosis with Heart Chakra work allows these blocks to be surfaced and gently reframed.
- **Example:** While hands rest over the client's chest, the practitioner guides them into a visualization of a green light or a rose blooming at the heart. Suggestions such as *"Your heart is safe to open,"* or *"You are free to give and receive love"* anchor the new heart-centered reality.

REFLEXOLOGY AND THE HEART

Reflexology maps the entire body onto the feet and hands. Specific points correspond to the heart and lungs — both directly connected to Anahata.

- **Heart Reflex Point:** Located on the left foot, just below the ball of the foot, near the center.
- **Lung Reflex Points:** Found just beneath the toes across the width of both feet.

- **Why it works with Anahata:** Stimulating these points clears stagnation in the physical organs linked with the Heart Chakra, while also moving blocked emotional energy.
- **Example:** Before or after a Reiki heart session, apply gentle pressure to the heart and lung reflexes, visualizing green light flowing up from the feet into the chest. This unites body-based therapy with energetic healing.

AROMATHERAPY AND THE HEART

Essential oils are one of the most direct ways to shift the emotional tone of the heart field because they influence the limbic system.

- **Rose Oil:** Opens and softens the heart, soothing grief.
- **Geranium Oil:** Restores emotional balance, especially after heartbreak.
- **Bergamot Oil:** Lifts mood and releases fear of rejection.
- **Why it works with Anahata:** When inhaled or applied over the sternum, oils infuse the heart field with vibrational support.
- **Example:** Diffuse rose and bergamot during a session. As the client breathes in, guide them to imagine the fragrance becoming a healing light that spreads through the chest.

PRACTICAL WAYS TO COMBINE MODALITIES

- **Hypnosis + Reiki:** Begin with Reiki hand placement over the chest, then guide the client into a heart-opening hypnotic visualization.
- **Reflexology + Aromatherapy:** Apply diluted rose oil to the heart reflex point on the foot, massaging with intention.
- **All Three Together:** Use a short hypnotic induction to bring the client into relaxation, apply reflexology on the

heart point, and diffuse geranium oil in the room while you channel Reiki to the chest.

THE HIDDEN GIFT OF INTEGRATION

When combined, these methods work like a symphony: hypnosis clears subconscious programs, reflexology grounds heart energy through the body, and aromatherapy creates a fragrant atmosphere of love and openness. The result is not just healing, but a **multisensory heart experience** that lingers long after the session ends.

Chapter 10 – Transformation Through Anahata

Case Studies: Grief Release, Self-Love Awakening, Relationship Healing

Theory and practices are powerful, but transformation becomes real when we see how the Heart Chakra responds in lived experience. The following case studies (based on composites of real scenarios) show how working with Anahata can create profound shifts in people's lives.

CASE STUDY 1: GRIEF RELEASE

The Story:
Maria, a 54-year-old woman, came to a Reiki session carrying deep grief after the passing of her partner. Her chest often felt heavy, and she described it as "a stone sitting on my heart."

The Session:
The practitioner focused on the heart and lung areas, using gentle Reiki hand placements over the sternum and upper back. Rose oil was diffused, and Maria was guided through a green light visualization, imagining her breath softening the "stone."

The Transformation:
Midway through the session, tears began to flow. She described feeling warmth spreading through her chest, as if "the stone was

melting." Over several sessions, her grief didn't vanish, but it softened. She began to speak of her partner with gratitude rather than only pain.

Lesson of Anahata:
The Heart Chakra does not erase grief — it transforms it into love, allowing loss to be carried with compassion instead of heaviness.

CASE STUDY 2: SELF-LOVE AWAKENING

The Story:
James, 32, struggled with self-criticism and low self-worth. He often said, "I'm not good enough," and had difficulty maintaining healthy boundaries.

The Session:
The practitioner combined Reiki with affirmations. As hands rested over James's chest, he was guided to repeat silently: *"I love myself. My heart radiates love."* Rose quartz was placed on his sternum, and a forgiveness breath exercise was used (inhale love, exhale self-judgment).

The Transformation:
James reported feeling a warmth he hadn't experienced before: "It felt like I was hugging myself from the inside." In the weeks following, he noticed he could speak up more confidently and treat himself with more kindness.

Lesson of Anahata:
When the heart opens inward, self-love becomes the soil where new confidence and boundaries can grow.

CASE STUDY 3: RELATIONSHIP HEALING

The Story:
Sofia and her partner had grown distant, locked in cycles of criticism and defensiveness. She came for sessions, hoping to "reopen her heart."

The Session:
During Reiki, the practitioner placed one hand on her heart and one hand on her throat — addressing both love and communication. She was guided through a rose meditation. visualizing her heart unfolding petal by petal. Essential oils of geranium and bergamot were used to encourage balance and joy.

The Transformation:
Sofia described a sudden wave of compassion for herself and her partner. In the weeks that followed, instead of reacting with criticism, she began pausing to listen. Conversations softened, and her relationship gradually shifted from tension to connection.

Lesson of Anahata:
The Heart Chakra restores harmony in relationships by reawakening compassion — reminding us to see others through the lens of love rather than fear.

WHY CASE STUDIES MATTER

Each story demonstrates a key truth: healing the heart doesn't mean avoiding pain, but meeting it with compassion. Whether it's grief, self-doubt, or relational conflict, Anahata provides the energy of transformation — turning heaviness into light. wounds into wisdom, and separation into connection.

Practitioner Stories of Breakthroughs in Reiki Sessions

Healing through the Heart Chakra doesn't only transforms the client — it also deeply touches the practitioner. Many Reiki healers describe moments in sessions where Anahata becomes a portal for breakthroughs that go far beyond technique.

BREAKTHROUGH 1: THE RELEASE OF HIDDEN GRIEF

Practitioner's Perspective:
"I had a client who carried a constant tightness in the chest. During Reiki, I placed one hand on the front of her heart and one between her shoulder blades. Suddenly, I felt an overwhelming heaviness in my own chest — like I wanted to cry. I held the space quietly, and a few minutes later, she began to sob. Afterward, she told me she had never cried after her mother's passing years ago. The session gave her permission to finally release it."

Lesson of Anahata: The heart doesn't always open with words — sometimes it needs safe silence and presence to let go.

BREAKTHROUGH 2: FROM NUMBNESS TO WARMTH

Practitioner's Perspective:
"One client said she couldn't 'feel' anything — no joy, no sadness, just numbness. As I worked over her heart, I visualized green light filling the space. Slowly, her breathing deepened. At the end, she told me, 'It felt like my chest was frozen, and now it's thawing.' It was the first time she had felt warmth in her heart in years."

Lesson of Anahata: Even when emotions are frozen, the heart remembers how to open when met with steady, compassionate energy.

BREAKTHROUGH 3: RELEASING FEAR OF LOVE

Practitioner's Perspective:
"A young man came in saying he was terrified of intimacy. When I scanned over his heart field, I felt sharp, jittery energy — like static. I held my hands a few inches away, using the aura-clearing protocol. Afterward, he shared that for the first time, he felt safe imagining himself in a relationship. He said, 'It's like the fear isn't gone, but it's not choking me anymore.'"

Lesson of Anahata: Healing doesn't always mean erasing fear — sometimes it's simply loosening its grip so love has space to breathe.

BREAKTHROUGH 4: PRACTITIONER'S OWN HEALING

Practitioner's Perspective:
"During a session, I suddenly felt my own heart ache while working on a client's grief. Instead of resisting, I allowed the energy to move through me, breathing deeply into my chest. Later, I realized I had also released my own hidden grief. Healing is never one-way — when we work with the heart, it heals both client and practitioner."

Lesson of Anahata: The healer is also healed. The heart field is shared, reminding us that love flows in both directions.

WHY THESE STORIES MATTER

These breakthroughs remind us that Reiki is not just a technique but a relationship — a meeting of hearts. The practitioner brings presence, intention, and compassion; the client brings openness and courage. Together, through Anahata, breakthroughs arise that transform lives in ways no method alone could create.

The Ripple Effect: How Opening the Heart Transforms Entire Energy Fields

When the Heart Chakra opens, the transformation doesn't stop at the individual. Anahata radiates like a sun — its energy moving through the aura, into the environment, and even into the lives of others. This ripple effect is one of the most profound aspects of heart-centered healing.

HOW THE HEART RADIATES

- **Electromagnetic Field:** The heart's field extends several feet beyond the body, influencing those nearby.
- **Emotional Resonance:** When your heart is open, others instinctively feel calmer, safer, and more receptive.
- **Energetic Harmony:** Anahata acts like a tuning fork, inviting other chakras and energy systems into balance.

THE RIPPLE WITHIN THE PRACTITIONER

When practitioners open their own hearts, they notice changes beyond the healing space:

- They feel more resilient under stress.
- Their relationships naturally soften, with less conflict and more patience.
- Intuitive insights become clearer, as if guided by love instead of fear.

THE RIPPLE IN THE CLIENT'S LIFE

Clients who experience heart-centered healing often report:

- Sudden shifts in how others respond to them — more kindness, openness, and connection.

- Resolution of conflicts or relationships begins to heal without direct effort.
- A new sense of vitality, creativity, or joy in daily life.

As one client said after a heart-opening Reiki session: *"It's like people around me started changing, but really, it was me — I was different."*

THE COLLECTIVE RIPPLE

When many hearts open, the ripple becomes a wave. Communities, families, and even groups of strangers can feel the effects of shared compassion. Spiritual traditions around the world affirm this truth: one heart opening in love lifts the vibration of all.

WHY THIS MATTERS FOR PRACTITIONERS

When you work with the Heart Chakra, you are never just healing one client — you are influencing the wider field they live in. Their family, their workplace, and their community all feel the subtle transformation.

Healing the heart is not only personal; it is **collective.** Every act of heart-centered presence adds to the greater resonance of compassion in the world.

184 | DR. CONSTANCE SANTEGO

Chapter 11 – Reflection & Integration

Daily Self-Care Rituals to Keep the Heart Open

Keeping the Heart Chakra open isn't about doing something once — it's about weaving small, intentional practices into everyday life. These rituals don't have to be long or complicated; the power lies in consistency. When practiced regularly, they keep your heart field soft, balanced, and resilient.

MORNING HEART CHECK-IN

Begin each day by placing your hand on your chest and taking three slow breaths. Ask yourself:

- *"How does my heart feel today?"*
- *"What does it need — comfort, courage, rest, or openness?"*

This simple check-in keeps you connected to your emotional state before the world pulls you in different directions.

AFFIRMATIONS OF LOVE

Words are vibrations that shape energy. Repeat a few heart-centered affirmations out loud or silently throughout the day:

- *"I am love. I am loved. I radiate love."*
- *"My heart is safe to open."*
- *"I give and receive love with ease."*

GREEN & PINK IMMERSION

Surround yourself with the colors of Anahata. Wear green clothing, place pink flowers on your desk, or eat leafy greens and berries. Color works directly on the subconscious and helps reinforce balance.

BREATH OF GRATITUDE

Pause once or twice a day to take five slow breaths, inhaling with the thought *"I receive love"* and exhaling with the thought *"I give love."* This resets the heart's rhythm and restores coherence.

ACTS OF COMPASSION

Choose one small act of kindness daily — send a kind message, hold space for someone, or even smile at a stranger. Compassion in action strengthens the heart field and keeps it open.

EVENING RELEASE RITUAL

Before bed, place your hand over your chest and silently say:

- *"I release today with love. I forgive myself and others. I rest in peace."*
  This clears emotional residue so your heart doesn't carry it into the next day.

Daily practices anchor Anahata in everyday reality. Instead of waiting for big breakthroughs, these rituals keep the heart gently open, reminding you that love is not just a feeling but a daily way of living.

Journaling Prompts for Forgiveness, Love, and Boundaries

Writing has the power to move energy from the heart onto the page, where it can be seen, released, and transformed. Use these prompts to explore and integrate the deeper lessons of Anahata.

Forgiveness

Forgiveness isn't about excusing harmful actions; it's about releasing the weight of carrying them in your heart. These prompts help open space for healing:

- Who or what still feels heavy in my heart? What would I like to let go of?
- What does forgiveness mean to me today? Is it possible to forgive without forgetting?
- Where might I need to forgive myself to feel lighter and freer?
- If I could write a letter of forgiveness (whether I send it or not), what would it say?

Love

Love begins within and radiates outward. Journaling about love helps you strengthen your connection to yourself, others, and the world:

- When do I feel most connected to love? What practices or people awaken that feeling?
- How do I express love to myself? How could I do this more often?
- Who in my life reminds me of unconditional love? What qualities do they show me?
- If love were speaking through me right now, what would it want to say?

Boundaries

Healthy boundaries are an essential part of an open heart — they protect love, rather than restrict it:

- Where in my life do I give too much without receiving enough in return?
- What situations or people leave me feeling drained? What boundary might I need here?
- How can I communicate "no" with love, clarity, and respect?
- What would my heart feel like if I honored my own needs as much as I honor others'?

HOW TO USE THESE PROMPTS

- Choose one area (forgiveness, love, or boundaries) to focus on each week.
- Free-write for 10–15 minutes, without worrying about grammar or structure.
- Revisit your answers after a month to notice shifts in your heart space.

Guided Exercise: Creating a Heart-Centered Life Mantra

A mantra is a short phrase or statement you repeat to align your mind, energy, and spirit with your deepest truth. For the Heart Chakra, a mantra becomes a compass — a reminder to live in love, balance, and compassion.

This exercise will help you craft a personal mantra that opens and strengthens your heart every time you speak it.

Step 1: Center in the Heart

- Sit quietly, place your hands over your chest, and take three deep breaths.
- Imagine a soft green or pink light glowing in your sternum.
- Ask silently: *"What does my heart most want me to remember?"*

Step 2: Choose Your Theme

Decide what your heart needs most right now:

- **Forgiveness:** letting go of past hurts.
- **Love:** strengthening compassion for self or others.
- **Boundaries:** honoring your worth.
- **Peace:** finding calm in daily life.
- **Unity:** feeling connected to something greater.

Step 3: Create Your Mantra

Write a simple, positive phrase in the present tense. Keep it short enough to repeat easily. For example:

- *"I am love, I radiate love."*

- *"My heart is safe to open."*
- *"I forgive and I am free."*
- *"I honor myself with love and respect."*
- *"I live from compassion and peace."*

Step 4: Empower It with Breath

- Inhale slowly through the nose.
- As you exhale, speak your mantra softly or silently.
- Repeat 7–10 times, letting the words sink into your heart field.

Step 5: Carry It Into Life

Use your mantra:

- **Morning ritual:** Repeat it as you wake up to set your energy for the day.
- **During stress:** Whisper it when emotions feel overwhelming.
- **Before bed:** Say it to release the day with love.

THE GIFT OF A HEART MANTRA

Your mantra is more than words — it's a vibration. Each time you repeat it, you retrain your heart to stay open, balanced, and connected. Over time, it becomes second nature — guiding you into a heart-centered life.

PRACTITIONER REFLECTION QUESTIONS FOR CONTINUED GROWTH

As a practitioner, your heart is not only the tool but also the teacher. Returning again and again to reflection ensures that your healing practice grows with integrity, compassion, and clarity. Use these questions as journal prompts or as quiet meditations after client sessions.

Self-Connection

- How do I know when my own Heart Chakra is open? What signs show up in my body, emotions, or energy field?
- Where in my personal life do I still struggle with forgiveness, love, or boundaries? How might this affect my work with clients?
- What daily rituals help me keep my own heart balanced and protected?

Client Connection

- In recent sessions, how did I sense my clients' heart energy? Through warmth, heaviness, images, or emotion?
- How do I hold space for clients without taking on their emotional burdens?
- When have I felt the most heart coherence with a client? What created that moment of resonance?

Professional Growth

- Am I practicing from a place of technique alone, or am I allowing my heart to lead?
- What breakthroughs have I witnessed in sessions that continue to shape my understanding of Anahata?
- Which modalities (Reiki, hypnosis, reflexology, aromatherapy, etc.) feel most natural for me to integrate with heart-centered healing?

The Bigger Picture

- How does my open heart ripple into my family, community, or the wider world?
- In what ways has working with the Heart Chakra changed *me* as a healer and as a human being?
- What is one heart-centered quality (compassion, patience, trust, etc.) I want to embody more fully in the months ahead?

HOW TO USE THESE QUESTIONS

- **Weekly:** Pick one question and explore it in writing for 10–15 minutes.
- **Monthly:** Revisit your answers — notice what has shifted or deepened.
- **Yearly:** Review your reflections as a map of your growth as a heart-centered practitioner.

Chapter 12 – Quick Reference Toolkit

HOW TO USE THIS TOOLKIT

These tables are designed as a **quick guide** — whether you're a practitioner preparing for a session, or simply doing your own daily practice. Pick one or two tools from each category to create a heart-centered routine:

- Morning: Affirmation + essential oil.
- Afternoon: Leafy greens + breathwork.
- Evening: Crystal meditation + heart-tuned music.

AFFIRMATIONS FOR THE HEART CHAKRA

Purpose	Affirmation
Self-love	*"I love and accept myself fully."*
Openness	*"My heart is safe to open."*
Balance	*"I give and receive love with ease."*
Healing	*"I forgive and release with compassion."*
Unity	*"I am connected to all of life through love."*

CRYSTALS FOR ANAHATA

Crystal	Quality	Best Use
Rose Quartz	Unconditional love, compassion	Place on chest during meditation
Emerald	Harmony, honesty, abundance	Wear over heart or in jewelry
Jade	Peace, protection, emotional balance	Carry in pocket, massage tools
Malachite	Transformation, releasing old wounds	Lay on chest to clear blockages
Rhodochrosite	Inner child healing, self-compassion	Hold during journaling or reflection

FOODS FOR THE HEART CHAKRA

Food Type	Examples	Benefits
Leafy Greens	Spinach, kale, arugula	Oxygenation, balance, vitality
Green Fruits & Veg	Cucumber, avocado, kiwi	Hydration, harmony
Herbs & Teas	Hawthorn, rose, mint, tulsi	Heart strength, grief release
Comfort Foods	Dark chocolate, honey, nuts	Joy, nurturing

ESSENTIAL OILS FOR HEART HEALING

Oil	Quality	How to Use
Rose	Highest vibration, opens unconditional love	Diffuse, anoint chest
Geranium	Emotional balance, softens grief	Massage oil, bath, diffuser
Bergamot	Joy, optimism, releases anxiety	Diffuse in morning, pulse points
Ylang-Ylang	Sensuality, eases jealousy	Anoint wrists, blend in perfume
Sandalwood	Spiritual peace, grounding	Meditation incense or chest rub

YOGA POSES FOR OPENING ANAHATA

Pose	Benefit
Camel (Ustrasana)	Deep chest expansion, courage, grief release
Bridge (Setu Bandhasana)	Energizes chest, calms mind
Cobra (Bhujangasana)	Confidence, warmth, gentle heart opener
Supported Fish (Matsyasana with props)	Passive heart opening, restores balance
Child's Pose (Arms extended)	Grounding, softens heart tension

FREQUENCIES & SOUND HEALING

Frequency	Tool	Effect
639 Hz	Tuning forks, sound tracks	Opens the heart, encourages love and harmony
YAM Mantra	Voice, chanting	Clears and activates the Heart Chakra
Singing Bowls (C/ F notes)	Bowls tuned to heart tones	Balances energy, releases grief

Practitioner Cheat-Sheet: Heart-Focused Reiki Sessions

Session Preparation

- **Center yourself:** Hands over heart, breathe slowly. repeat: *"I am a clear channel of love and healing."*
- **Set intention:** Hold the client in compassion. Invite their heart to open safely.
- **Create atmosphere:** Diffuse rose/geranium oil, place rose quartz nearby, play soft music (639 Hz).

Core Hand Positions

1. **Front Heart:** One hand over sternum.
2. **Back Heart:** One hand between shoulder blades.
   - Option: "Sandwich" — both positions held together.
3. **Aura Sweep:** Hover hands 2–6 inches over chest, clearing stagnant energy in circles.

4. **Expansion Motion:** Hands start at chest, slowly move outward (like opening curtains).

Session Flow (Approx. 20–30 minutes on heart area)

1. **Scan:** Sense heaviness, temperature shifts, or emotional impressions in chest field.
2. **Hold:** Place hands gently on front/back heart for 3–5 minutes.
3. **Clear:** Sweep aura, shake off stagnant energy. Replace with green/pink light.
4. **Expand:** Visualize the heart glowing outward, connecting client to love.
5. **Integrate:** Return to sternum, breathe with client until energy feels steady.
6. **Ground:** Finish by placing hands on feet or hips.

Cues of Release

- Deep sighs, tears, laughter.
- Warmth or tingling in chest.
- Client reports images, memories, or feelings of lightness.

Affirmations to Suggest

- *"My heart is safe to open."*
- *"I forgive and I am free."*
- *"I am love, I am loved."*

Quick Add-Ons

- **Crystal:** Place rose quartz or jade on chest.
- **Breathwork:** Guide inhale with *"receive love"*, exhale with *"give love."*
- **Sound:** Chant *YAM* softly or play 639 Hz tones.

Closing the Session

- Thank the client's heart for its willingness to heal.
- Invite them to take 3 breaths into their chest.
- Suggest post-session journaling: *"What is my heart ready to release? What is it ready to welcome?"*

Daily 5-Minute Heart Opening Routine

This short practice combines breath, touch, visualization, and intention. Do it in the morning to start your day, or anytime you feel your heart closing.

Minute 1: Centering Breath

- Sit comfortably with your spine tall.
- Place one or both hands over your sternum.
- Inhale slowly through the nose, exhale gently through the mouth.
- Focus your attention on the rise and fall of your chest.

Minute 2: Heart Visualization

- Imagine a soft green light glowing in the center of your chest.
- With each inhale, see it expand like a gentle sun.
- With each exhale, imagine it radiating outward, filling your body with warmth.

Minute 3: Gratitude Focus

- Think of one person, moment, or gift you are grateful for.
- Allow that gratitude to rest in your heart, fueling the green light.
- If emotion arises, let it flow without judgment.

Minute 4: Affirmation

Choose one phrase and repeat it with each breath:

- *"My heart is safe to open."*
- *"I am love, I radiate love."*
- *"I forgive and I am free."*

Minute 5: Heart Extension

- Visualize your heart's light extending a few feet beyond your body.
- Imagine it touching the room, your loved ones, or even the world.
- End with one deep breath, whispering: *"I carry this love into my day."*

Why This Works

Five minutes is enough to reset your nervous system, calm emotional tension, and re-align with love. Done daily, this routine gradually rewires the heart to remain open, resilient, and connected.

Conclusion: Living Through the Heart

The Heart Chakra is the meeting point of opposites — body and soul, giving and receiving, human and divine. As we have explored, it is the bridge that connects all other chakras, reminding us that no healing is complete without love at the center.

By learning to open, balance, and protect Anahata, you not only transform your own life but also create ripples of healing in your relationships, your community, and even the collective heart of humanity. Love is not just an emotion but an energy — one that can be cultivated, expanded, and shared.

Remember:

- Every breath into the heart is a step toward peace.
- Every act of forgiveness is a clearing of old wounds.
- Every choice to love, even when difficult, is a victory of the soul.

As you continue your journey, may your heart remain your compass, guiding you to live with compassion, courage, and connection.

Looking Ahead: The Next Step in the Chakra Journey

Though the heart is central, it cannot stand alone. The lower chakras — the **Base (Root), Sacral, and Solar Plexus** — form the foundation that supports the heart's opening.

- **The Root Chakra (Muladhara):** The grounding force of safety, stability, and belonging. Without this root, the heart cannot feel secure enough to open.

- **The Sacral Chakra (Svadhisthana):** The seat of creativity, pleasure, and emotional flow. When balanced, it allows love to be joyful and expressive.
- **The Solar Plexus Chakra (Manipura):** The center of willpower, confidence, and personal identity. It empowers love to be strong, clear, and courageous.

In the next books of this series, we will travel downward into these foundational centers, uncovering how they shape not only our survival but also our ability to live fully and love deeply. Just as a tree needs strong roots and a firm trunk to support blossoming branches, your heart needs the grounding and vitality of the lower chakras to truly thrive.

So as you close this book, take with you the light of Anahata — and prepare to step into the next phase of your journey: discovering the wisdom of the Root Chakra and building a foundation strong enough to support the fullness of love.

Bibliography

CLASSICAL & YOGIC SOURCES

- Feuerstein, Georg. *The Yoga Tradition: Its History, Literature, Philosophy, and Practice.* Hohm Press, 2001.
- Avalon, Arthur (Sir John Woodroffe). *The Serpent Power: The Secrets of Tantric and Shaktic Yoga.* Dover Publications, 1974.
- Swami Sivananda. *The Chakras.* Divine Life Society, 1994.
- Upanishads (trans. Eknath Easwaran). *The Upanishads.* Nilgiri Press, 2007.

CHAKRA & ENERGY HEALING WORKS

- Judith, Anodea. *Wheels of Life: A User's Guide to the Chakra System.* Llewellyn Publications, 1987.
- Myss, Caroline. *Anatomy of the Spirit.* Harmony Books, 1996.
- Brennan, Barbara Ann. *Hands of Light: A Guide to Healing Through the Human Energy Field.* Bantam, 1988.
- Sills, Franklyn. *Foundations in Craniosacral Biodynamics: The Breath of Life and Fundamental Skills.* North Atlantic Books, 2012.

REIKI & SPIRITUAL HEALING

- Takata, Hawayo. *Reiki: Hawayo Takata's Story.* Reiki Alliance, 1998.

- Petter, Frank Arjava. *This Is Reiki: Transformation of Body, Mind and Soul from the Origins to the Practice.* Lotus Press, 2012.
- Rand, William Lee. *Reiki: The Healing Touch.* Vision Publications, 1991.

CROSS-CULTURAL & MYSTICAL REFERENCES

- Halevi, Z'ev ben Shimon. *Kabbalah: Tradition of Hidden Knowledge.* Thames & Hudson, 1991.
- Hanh, Thich Nhat. *Peace Is Every Step.* Bantam, 1992.
- Ibn Arabi. *Journey to the Lord of Power.* Inner Traditions, 1981.
- Underhill, Evelyn. *Mysticism: A Study in the Nature and Development of Spiritual Consciousness.* Dover Publications, 2002.

MODERN SCIENCE & RESEARCH

- McCraty, Rollin, et al. *Science of the Heart: Exploring the Role of the Heart in Human Performance.* HeartMath Institute, 2015.
- Childre, Doc, and Howard Martin. *The HeartMath Solution.* HarperOne, 1999.
- Pert, Candace B. *Molecules of Emotion: The Science Behind Mind-Body Medicine.* Scribner, 1997.
- Lipton, Bruce H. *The Biology of Belief.* Hay House, 2005.

ADDITIONAL RESOURCES

- Eden, Donna. *Energy Medicine.* TarcherPerigee, 2008.
- Osho. *The Book of Secrets: 112 Meditations to Discover the Mystery Within.* St. Martin's Griffin, 1998.
- Chopra, Deepak. *Quantum Healing.* Bantam, 19

Message From The Author

Dear Reader,

As you close the final pages of this book, I want to pause and thank you — not only for reading, but for being willing to take this journey into your own heart. Writing *Heart Chakra 101* has reminded me again and again that healing is never just intellectual. It is lived. It is breathed. And it is shared.

The heart is where so many of our joys, wounds, and questions meet. It is the place that aches when life breaks us open, and the place that shines when we allow love to flow freely. I chose to begin this series with the Heart Chakra because, without love at the center, all other work — whether with body, mind, or spirit — remains incomplete.

If there is one message I hope stays with you, it is this: **Your heart is stronger than you think, softer than you fear, and wiser than you imagine.** Every time you open it, even just a little, you create ripples of healing that touch more lives than you will ever know.

This book is not the end, but a beginning. Ahead, we will journey into the lower chakras — the Root, Sacral, and Solar Plexus — exploring how safety, creativity, and personal power form the foundation that allows the heart to blossom fully. Each chakra tells a part of your story, and together they weave the map of your wholeness.

From my heart to yours, thank you for walking this path with me. May this work support you in creating a life of balance, compassion, and connection. And may your heart always guide you home.

With love and light,
Dr. Constance Santego

About the Author

Dr. Constance Santego, Ph.D., DNM is an award-winning author, teacher, and natural medicine doctor who has dedicated

more than 25 years to the study and practice of energy healing. A Grand Reiki Master and founder of multiple wellness and educational programs, she has trained thousands of students worldwide in Reiki, holistic therapies, and intuitive development.

Her passion is to bring ancient wisdom into practical, modern tools that anyone can use for healing and self-discovery. She has authored more than forty books, ranging from the *Reiki*

Wisdom series and *Secrets of a Healer* guides to spiritual fiction exploring the Nine Spiritual Gifts. Her teaching blends Eastern philosophies, Western natural medicine, and modern energy science — always with compassion at the center.

Dr. Santego's mission is to help people connect with their inner wisdom, awaken their intuitive gifts, and live with greater balance, joy, and love. When she is not writing or teaching, she enjoys life in British Columbia, surrounded by nature's beauty, which continues to inspire her work.

ALSO AVAILABLE

For additional information on

Constance Santego's

wide range of Motivational Products, Coaching Sessions,
Spiritual Retreats,
Live Events and Educational Programs

Go to

www.ConstanceSantego.ca

Follow on Instagram - Constance_Santego and
Facebook - constancesantegoo

Subscribe and receive Free Information and Meditations on her
YouTube Channel - Constance Santego

Secrets of a Healer, Magic of Reiki

ISBN: 978-1-7772220-0-0

www.ingramcontent.com/pod-product-compliance
Lightning Source LLC
Chambersburg PA
CBHW071727120626

46550CB00002B/412